GRIEF

EMPOWERING YOU

The Rowman & Littlefield Empowering You series is aimed to help you, as a young adult, deal with important topics that you, your friends, or family might be facing. Whether you are looking for answers about certain illnesses, social issues, or personal problems, the books in this series provide you with the most up-to-date information. Throughout each book you will also find stories from other teenagers to provide personal perspectives on the subject.

GRIEF

Insights and Tips for Teenagers

JOE JANSEN

ROWMAN & LITTLEFIELD
Lanham • Boulder • New York • London

Published by Rowman & Littlefield
An imprint of The Rowman & Littlefield Publishing Group, Inc.
4501 Forbes Boulevard, Suite 200, Lanham, Maryland 20706
www.rowman.com

6 Tinworth Street, London, SE11 5AL, United Kingdom

British Library Cataloguing in Publication Information Available

Library of Congress Cataloging-in-Publication Data

Names: Jansen, Joe, 1961– author.
Title: Grief : insights and tips for teenagers / Joe Jansen.
Description: Lanham : Rowman & Littlefield, 2020. | Series: Empowering you |
    Includes bibliographical references and index. | Audience: Grades
    10–12 | Summary: "This book is a valuable resource for teenagers who may
    be experiencing grief due to the loss of a friend or family member. It
    provides insights to help them understand what they are going through
    and includes tips and resources from both experts and young adults on
    how to cope with their grief"— Provided by publisher.
Identifiers: LCCN 2020033373 (print) | LCCN 2020033374 (ebook) | ISBN
    9781538136928 (paperback) | ISBN 9781538136935 (ebook)
Subjects: LCSH: Grief—Juvenile literature. | Grief in
    adolescence—Juvenile literature. | Loss (Psychology)—Juvenile
    literature.
Classification: LCC BF575.G7.J366 2020 (print) | LCC BF575.G7 (ebook) |
    DDC 155.9/370835—dc23
LC record available at https://lccn.loc.gov/2020033373
LC ebook record available at https://lccn.loc.gov/2020033374

CONTENTS

ACKNOWLEDGMENTS

If this book has been helpful to young people working through the grief of losing someone they love, I hope it has been due to the voices of the six fine teenagers and young adults who agreed to share their stories here.

I'm grateful to Kate for talking about how hard she worked to care for her brother and sisters, before and after her mother's death, while she also worked to heal and care for herself. Logan made me laugh with his story of listening to country music in the cab of the pickup he inherited from his dad and hearing his father's objection to "that music." Dexter inspired me with his insistence on placing his dad's urn in a place of honor and lacing his boots with his father's laces.

I appreciated hearing Bailey's efforts to create a STEM program for girls in local elementary schools, in her scientist-sister's memory. Grace lifted me up with her stories of how performing in musical theater lifted her up, and her devotion to her younger brother and older sister. JDB showed courage in overcoming a reluctance to share his stories, and in our conversation raised his wrist to show his father's paracord and leather bracelets, which he now wore with pride in his father's memory.

I am grateful to the six of you, my young friends, for your courage and insights and willingness to help other young people by sharing the stories of your grief journeys. Some of you were of an age that required a parent's permission, and I express my appreciation to Jennifer (Logan's mom), Margaret (Grace's mother), Maura (Bailey's mom), and Mary (JDB's mother). Thanks to each of you for allowing me the privilege of speaking with your teenage son or daughter, and trusting me to respect and care for their feelings while bringing out stories that might help other kids.

For their introductions to some of these young people and their families, I express my appreciation to Jana DeCristofaro, LCSW, Community Response Program coordinator at the Dougy Center, in Portland, Oregon. The resources provided by the Dougy Center, including Jana's podcast, *Grief Out Loud*, are tools that can help kids and parents, regardless of where they live.

Thanks to Carol Braden, LMHC, clinical director of programs and services, and Tara Ntumba, LMHC, support group director, both from Brooke's Place for Grieving Young People, in Indianapolis, Indiana. The warm conversations, the introductions to teens who have grown because of the services you provide, and your invitation to the twentieth anniversary gathering for Brooke's Place all helped make this book happen.

My appreciation to Paul N. George, MS, LCSW, LMFT, of Living Well in Good Company, in Indianapolis, Indiana, for his insights into the grieving process and the use of EMDR therapy to facilitate healthy mourning.

To Rowman & Littlefield Publishers, I offer my appreciation for the opportunity to tell these stories. Thanks to acquisitions editors Stephen Ryan and Christen Karniski, and editorial assistant Erinn Slanina. Thanks also for the support of project editors Christopher Rivera and RoseMary Ludt.

To Audrey, who I met before she was born.

I also offer my thanks to my wife Jill for her patience and encouragement as I tried to tell these stories well.

YOU ARE NOT ALONE

Every book is guaranteed to have a final chapter. In every movie, the credits will roll. In every soccer match, the time runs out. In these lives we're given, our one guarantee is that our time is finite. It's true for ourselves, and it's true for every single person we know and love. Some of those people we love will leave here before us. Sometimes, they will die too soon, and that's going to hurt.

When you lose someone close to you, it might feel like you're all alone. A young girl who lost her mother described it as feeling like she was alone in a bubble. You may feel like you are stranded on the surface of some alien planet—separated from the person you lost or cut off from your friends who you think won't understand you. In all of this, there's good news: You don't have to do this by yourself. You're not alone.

You probably know the story of Lewis and Clark, the explorers who led an expedition in the early 1800s that blazed a trail through the American wilderness—from St. Louis to the Pacific Ocean and back. When they returned, they had maps to show others the way. When it comes to navigating grief and loss, other kids have been on the path you're on now, or at least a similar path that crosses the same kind of scary wilderness. If there's a dark forest to enter, other teens have entered that forest before you. They can tell you where the wolves are and how to make it through.

In this wilderness, are there raging rapids to cross? Other kids have stood on the banks of that river and can tell you how they got across without getting swept downstream. If they did get knocked off their feet and into fast water, they can tell you how they maneuvered to the bank and found a branch to grab. Other teens can tell you how they pulled themselves out, built a fire and dried their clothes, and were able to keep going.

On the Lewis and Clark Expedition, William Clark didn't cross the Rocky Mountains as a party of one. Meriwether Lewis wasn't by himself when he negotiated with Native American chiefs for safe passage. Lewis and Clark were not alone—more than thirty other explorers were in their party. Some hunted and kept the group fed. Some navigated, and some kept the expedition's records. The Shoshone woman Sacagawea helped translate, and her presence as a woman smoothed out the tense first meetings with newly encountered Native American tribes.

No single member of the Lewis and Clark Expedition ventured solo into the wilds. They were a corps. They made it through, and they found their way back home—together. On your journey of loss, you don't have to figure this out all by yourself, either. Other kids have lost someone they love. They've been in the same kind of wilderness as you might find yourself now. They've entered a dark wood and have come out on the other side. They've left maps for you. Those maps are here.

You'll meet some of these teens on the following pages. They're kids who've walked the path you're walking, who have faced the deaths of people they love and have worked forward through the grief that comes with that loss. They've agreed to share their experiences and their hopes. They talk about what has worked for them, what they wish they might have done differently, and about their hope for finding meaning in the future.

None of them will tell you how you should act, or what your grief should look like, or how you should find your way through your dark wilderness. One kid might beat the snot out of a punching bag, which gives her some sense of release. Another might find her solace on a long bike ride. A third teenager may find peace in the woods, walking a trail and hunting with his little brother, like they used to do with their dad.

Let's meet the teens who will be sharing their stories and personal journeys with you. You might think of us sitting around a table or a campfire together. As you can imagine, sharing their perspectives was not easy for them. Each of them agreed to talk about their experiences because they wanted to help you. Even though they don't know your name, or where are you grew up, or who you've lost, they all expressed the same sentiment: a desire to help other teens feel less alone.

The teenagers interviewed for this book expressed a sense of meaning and purpose in being able to offer their insights. They were eager to share what their challenges have been, what they've learned on their grief journeys, how they've grown and been able to find a way to live with meaning and purpose. They each said, in different ways, that some of that sense of meaning was coming from being able to help other kids who are also walking a path of loss and grief.

We'll let them introduce themselves.

KATE

"I'm Kate. I'm twenty now, but I was thirteen when my mom Stacey died in an accident. She had a lot of issues with addiction and mental illness, which often put me in the position of being a pseudo-mom and having to take care of my three younger siblings."

LOGAN

"My name is Logan. I'm eighteen now, and my dad's name was Marcus. He worked in an office for a while, then in a motorcycle shop that sold Harleys, Indians, and Hondas. After that, he was a stay-at-home dad with us. I was thirteen years old when he died in 2015. He'd had his share of health problems. The day he and my mom got married was the two-week anniversary of his kidney transplant. He was age forty-six when he had a heart attack."

DEXTER

"I'm Dexter, and I'm nineteen. Originally, I'm from Ukraine. I'm adopted, and my mom and dad decided to get me when I was about one. They lived in New Mexico at the time. They were the classic college couple, you know, both psychologists and both smart. We moved to Oregon when I was about eight. A couple of months after I turned sixteen, my dad William was sixty-six, and he passed away from a blood clot in his leg."

BAILEY

"My name is Bailey. My sister Sydney died a year and a half ago when she took her own life. She was my best friend and a huge role model. She taught me to love science and to help others around me. She lived in Africa and worked with a Belgian company that trained African giant pouched rats to sniff out land mines in war-torn countries, which was very inspiring. She was very intelligent, goofy, beautiful, and weird."

GRACE

"I'm Grace. I'm thirteen, and I was four years old when my dad Kenneth died. I don't remember a lot about him, and so it wasn't like I had him and then lost him. My older sister was nine when our dad died. For her, she has more memories of him than I do. For me, losing my dad is missing someone I never had."

JDB

"My friends call me JDB. I'm age fifteen. My dad's name was Brad. From the time I was little, we had three sports we'd always play together: football, basketball, and baseball. He was usually the coach or involved somehow. We also did martial arts together. I have good memories of changing in the backseat of his car between different events. My parents were older when they had me. I found my dad at home after he had a heart attack."

If it's okay with you in the pages ahead, we'll refer to Kate, Logan, Dexter, Bailey, Grace, and JDB collectively as "our friends." As we take this walk together, maybe you'll feel a connection, maybe hear some of your own experience in theirs, or find some insights in their vulnerability and honesty. Whether you're reading this in your bedroom or on your back porch, in a comfortable chair in your house, or slung in an Eno in the shade between two trees, you'll hopefully hear some perspectives from our friends that could be helpful. While they each have their own stories, they're open and willing to be honest. They'd each tell you that things are forever different now. It's going to hurt, and it will always hurt. But it will get better.

Our friends would probably also let you know that as long as you're willing to reach out and connect with kindred spirits, you will never have to walk this path alone.

PART I

UNDERSTANDING GRIEF

It's only three words, so it seems a simple question: "What is grief?" There may have been a day when you could have given a simple answer to that question. "Grief? I don't know. I guess it's sadness, right? But maybe like real heavy sadness?"

It's not until we experience the death of someone we love—a mother or a grandfather or a brother or a best friend—that we begin to see that grief is a lot more complicated than that. Grief doesn't fit cleanly into any one box. It can be a whole constellation of emotions: disbelief, deep sadness and longing, anger, guilt, and a feeling that you might be able to bargain your way out of this bad dream that's befallen you.

All those feelings can get swirled together and overlap with each other. You may feel sad and disbelieving that you've actually lost your brother and then find yourself angry at him for leaving you. Then you might feel guilty about feeling angry. Then maybe you feel even sadder trying to understand how you're supposed to deal with all these emotions at once. It can be a spiral.

Maybe the simplest way to define grief is that it's your mind and body's response to losing something important, and it's something that our evolution has given us to protect us while we start to get things figured out. Think about it like this: We've been human for maybe two hundred or three hundred thousand years now. For ten thousand generations, we've loved family and friends. For all those millennia, we've experienced grief as those people we love die. If the sadness of loss was something that incapacitated us for years or lifetimes, we wouldn't have survived as a people. Grief is something that our nature has given us to protect us emotionally and physically for some time—to let us heal and then to allow us to keep moving.

We've learned something along those hundreds of thousands of years. Our bodies and minds know that when the sun rises in the morning, we'll wake up. It's not something we need to think about; our bodies just wake up with the sunrise (even though an alarm clock sometimes does come in handy). When we jump in a cold lake, our muscles start to shiver as they work to warm us up—we don't have to "make ourselves shiver." When we skin a knee or get a cut, we don't have to think our cuts into stopping bleeding or knitting the flesh together to heal. We don't have to think about it—our bodies already know what to do.

We can similarly think of grief. There's a level of us deep down that knows how to grieve and how grieving can help us heal. We've been doing it for a quarter million years. Like we know that wrapping a blanket around us can help us stop shivering, there's a part of us that knows that having someone wrap their arms around us can help us bear the pain of grief.

Grief is also a process of redefining your sense of self. You haven't only lost a best friend or a parent or a brother or sister, but you've lost part of yourself too. If your mother dies, what happens to that part of you that is her daughter? Now that she's gone, who are you? What happens to that part of yourself that only she knew? What happens to your ideas about your future as you thought it would look? The process of grieving is part of what gives you the chance to redefine or rewrite your sense of who you are now without your person who died. That experience of trying to understand what grief is can be the start of a healing journey.

The journey of grief is also a paradox: it's at the same time both the most personal thing we can ever experience and a universal experience we all have as humans. On the one hand, nobody in the world ever had the same relationship you had with the person who died. The memories and knowledge of what the two of you shared belong only to you. Maybe you could put your memories into words, but words can only be reflections of what you feel in your grief—and it can feel like this kind of loss has never happened to anyone else before.

We have very few guarantees in life, and one of those guarantees is that life has a beginning and an end. Every single person we've ever known, and who we will know, will someday die. As long as we live and as long as we choose to love the people around us, we'll inevitably experience the sadness of loss when the lives of others come to an end. It's a universal truth that love can endure, but grief is the price of losing the person. Grief is the price of love.

CHAPTER ONE

GRIEF IS A HERO'S JOURNEY

You probably know the *Star Wars* movies. When George Lucas started writing those stories, he leaned heavily on the work of a teacher and mythologist named Joseph Campbell. Campbell was big on a type of story he called "the hero's journey." Different versions of the hero's journey appear in stories in all cultures on every continent. You can see the hero's journey in stories you've probably studied in school: *Beowulf* tells of a hero's journey. The Buddha's story is a hero's journey. *Harry Potter* is the tale of a hero's journey.

What does Harry Potter or Luke Skywalker have to do with the grief you're feeling right now? Here it is: in the grief you're feeling, you have embarked on a hero's journey yourself. Campbell mapped out the stages of the hero's journey. There are twelve stages (you can do a web search to find out more about them), but we can simplify it here and draw a parallel to *Star Wars*, just to illustrate.

At the beginning of the hero's journey, we're in our "ordinary life." Luke Skywalker, an ordinary kid, is doing his chores on the farm, where he lives with his aunt Beru and uncle Owen. You are a teenager doing everyday teenage stuff. Then something happens that changes everything and throws us out of our "ordinary world." Luke finds a hidden distress call from a mysterious woman who points him toward a struggle. The death of someone you dearly love upends your world.

Then there's a rejection or denial of the call. Luke says, "I can't go to Alderaan! I have moisture-farming chores to do!" Given a choice, you'd surely reject being pitched out of the normal world you inhabited before your parent, sibling, or best friend died.

5

From there, the hero's journey involves crossing a threshold. Luke leaves Tatooine to figure out how to be a Jedi; you embark on a journey to figure out who you are and how in the world you're supposed to live without your person in your life.

The hero's journey involves meeting a mentor: Luke gets guidance from Obi-Wan and Yoda. You will find those people who can help you along your path (they probably won't look like Jedi knights, but they're likely to have some wisdom and knowledge about the path you face). The hero's journey involves trials and battles, suffering, and having to confront the darkness (often in a cave).

Then Luke (you) undergoes an ordeal where a part of the old you is left behind, and there's a rebirth of a new you. In *Star Wars*, it's the scene where Luke shuts down his computer while he's making his run at the Death Star. With Darth Vader in hot pursuit, he leaves behind his dependence on machines and "uses the Force." In his triumph, he has evolved and becomes something new. For you, "using the Force" might be a point where something happens in your grief process where you're able to find "a new hope."

There's a final stage in the hero's journey that might apply here too. It's the stage where the hero returns to the world, now having mastered her inner and outer worlds. Mastering the fear of death, the hero now has the freedom to live fully and with less fear. The hero also returns carrying gifts; she's able to share what she's learned with the rest of the people.

It's possible to think of our friends—Kate, Dexter, JDB, Bailey, Logan, and Grace—as guides like that. None of them would call themselves "heroes," but each of them has been on a hero's journey. They were thrown out of their old lives and faced challenges with the help of their mentors and guides. Each of them has met his or her darkness and found a way forward. Just as with "the return of the hero," they're willing to share what they know about their journeys.

Does it feel like there may be some parallels between this ancient mythological story of "the hero's journey" and the grief journey you're on? The idea is not so much to think of yourself as a hero (though you may well end up being a hero to other people down the road). It's to recognize that in working through your grief, you are embarking on a path that humans have tread before you for thousands of years. You're not the first one to walk this path, and you don't have to walk it alone. One of Campbell's books is titled *The Hero with a Thousand Faces*; the hero's face appears in stories everywhere, in all cultures across time. In that book, Campbell says of our individual hero's journey:

> We have not even to risk the adventure alone, for the heroes of all time have gone before us. The labyrinth is thoroughly known . . . we have only to follow the thread of the hero path. And where we had thought to find an abomination, we shall find a God.
>
> And where we had thought to slay another, we shall slay ourselves. Where we had thought to travel outwards, we shall come to the center of our own existence. And where we had thought to be alone, we shall be with all the world.

We're all on a hero's journey. Each milestone of our lives is crossing a boundary where the unknown lies on the other side: such as a bar mitzvah, getting a driver's license, seeing your body change as you leave adolescence, graduating from elementary school and entering high school, graduating from high school and going off to college or work or whatever comes next.

The hero's journey story appears everywhere because it's ingrained in our human experience. Experiencing grief is part of that universal human journey. Every single one of us will experience the death of someone close to us. If we open ourselves to love, we will eventually feel the experience of loss and the grief that goes along with that loss. It's part of our experience on this earth.

Just as there are "thoroughly known" stages of a hero's journey (as Campbell said), some different stages of grief have been well understood too. Disbelief, anger, bargaining, deep sadness, acceptance, and finding a sense of meaning and purpose are stages of the grief process that author David Kessler has described, which he and grief expert Elisabeth Kübler-Ross describe in their work together.

The stages of grief are not a ladder or levels in a game, where you pass "Level Disbelief," leaving that behind for "Level Anger." Kessler says, "Stages are not a map. They reflect where you are."

CHAPTER TWO

DISBELIEF

Disbelief is likely to be the first of many stages that we experience when someone we love dies. It's a natural form of self-protection. It's nature's way of slowing things down and giving us time to process the enormity of the unimaginable thing that's just happened to us. Our minds are giving us some space, so everything doesn't hit us all at once.

There's a physical parallel to "disbelief" that you might recognize. Have you ever walked through a dark room at night and accidentally banged your knee against a table or stubbed your toe? You know you just made contact, and maybe you even heard a smack as you connected. Have you noticed how the pain, though, doesn't hit right away? There's a second or maybe two before the signal makes it from your stubbed toe up to your brain. It's a grace period before you feel that sharp pain. You might have even said to yourself, "Uh-oh. Here it comes." Disbelief or denial can serve the same purpose. It gives us a moment to breathe to prepare us for what comes next. Disbelief is also our mind's first response to wanting to keep things the same and not wanting to deal with the idea that our mother or best friend or brother might be gone for good.

Logan and Bailey and some of our other friends talked about their own experiences of disbelief. It can be helpful to know that nobody's experience was exactly the same. No matter where or how the death occurred, the disbelief and the desire to deny that this unthinkable thing happened can be just as strong.

9

DEXTER

When Dexter came home from school and found his dad passed away in the front seat of his car, he said, "At first, I felt like 'no way this has happened!' This is not really real." Even as Dexter went through many other emotions around his grief, he would often return to a sense of disbelief. "Even months later, I'd feel like maybe he wasn't really gone," Dexter said. "Like maybe he's just off somewhere else. Then you just feel a lot of sorrow, and feel like 'I can't let this be!'"

BAILEY

The experience of disbelief was different for Bailey. Her sister died eight thousand miles away in Tanzania. She said that being separated by such great distance made the disbelief more intense. She said, "I definitely had a lot of disbelief, and I think it continues even today. When my sister took her life, she was living in Africa and working with a company that trained rats to sniff out land mines. Because I didn't live with her, it sometimes just feels like I'm 'just not with her at the moment,' but somewhere she's still alive. When I first found out that she'd taken her own life, I felt destroyed. I really didn't believe it was real."

Disbelief doesn't always just take the form of flat-out rejection of unwanted news. Sometimes, our minds might craft an alternative explanation to give us a little buffer between the reality and the pain that will soon follow it. If our person died in an auto accident, we might try to believe that maybe they were misidentified. If our person died after a course of chemo in the hospital, perhaps the nurses mixed up the records.

LOGAN

Logan talked about how his disbelief manifested when he got the news that his dad had died while his mom was running him to the hospital. "I'd gone to bed early the night before," Logan said.

"When I came downstairs that next morning, the first thing I saw was my grandfather. At the time, my dad and his parents weren't getting along. So, to see my grandfather in our house, I immediately knew something was not right. He just said, 'Your dad . . .'" Logan said, "I'd never seen my grandfather cry. Ever. Did I think my dad was dead? No. But if my grandfather was here, I knew it must be bad. I figured maybe my dad was just sick and in bad shape at the hospital or something. But that wasn't the case. I was only thirteen years old."

Disbelief or denial isn't something that shows up only at the news of your person's death and then fades away to be replaced by other "stages" of grief. The disbelief can show up again unexpectedly, even weeks or months after your person has died. It might hit you one afternoon when you're walking in after school and expect to see your sister sitting at the kitchen table doing her homework like she always did. Or you might hear a song that was your mom's favorite and can't believe she's not around so she can sing along.

Just like all the different phases of the grieving process, disbelief about the fact that your person has really died can be mixed in with other emotions.

JDB

JDB was able to find the self-awareness of how his thoughts and feelings overlapped each other. He said, "For me, the denial came along with the depression. But the two didn't come one after the other—they kind of came all together. Not at the same time, but in the same time frame. Different emotions were all right there together." JDB was able to recognize the sense of disbelief, to let himself experience it, and to find his way forward. "The denial was pretty bad," he said. "After a while, I was able to see that you have to start by accepting the truth that he's gone. Otherwise, how can you ever solve anything?"

It helps to know that the feeling of disbelief is a natural part of the grieving process. Think of it as your mind's momentary anesthesia, a pain reliever to lessen the shock of recognizing that things are going to be different now. You'll eventually begin to accept the reality of your loss, and that's the first of many steps along a path toward healing.

CHAPTER THREE

ANGER

The feeling of anger is something that often surprises teenagers who are experiencing grief. How could we feel anger? Isn't grief more about sadness? Yes, sadness is a big part of the grief experience, but there are lots of reasons that feelings of anger can arise. If we had a brother who died by overdose, it would make sense to feel angry with him for the decision he made. If we had a dad who died of a heart attack, maybe we'd feel mad that he didn't eat better, or exercise, or go to the doctor for checkups more often.

BAILEY

Anger might feel uncomfortable to express, but it's a natural part of the process that we need to let flow through us. Bailey has experienced anger around her sister taking her own life. "I have felt anger towards Sydney for leaving me, but then I feel guilty about those feelings," she said. Feeling angry and then feeling guilty about your anger isn't unusual. Lots of teens have feelings like that.

GRACE

Grace talked about the mix of emotions that she's felt, with anger being part of that mix. She said, "There are so many adjectives I could use to describe how grief feels. You can feel angry at your person because they left you, even if it wasn't their decision. Then you can feel empty or sad. Then there's a longing for someone who's just not there. Sometimes you can go from crying to angry to feeling empty and then back again. It can go back and forth, but it helps to know that all of it is part of experiencing grief."

LOGAN

Logan said that the grieving process was hard for him. He said it was a real churn of emotions, which included anger at his dad for dying. He said, "It's hard to describe all the emotions. The first thing I'd say is that it's hell. But all the emotions were such a mix: I was everything. I was sad. I was extremely angry. I was happy. Then I'd get angry again. I was everything. I found myself screaming and yelling at my dad. I'd be cussing him out and calling him a coward and yelling, 'You're not done yet!'"

Sometimes the circumstances of your person's death might mean that emotions like anger get put aside for a time, or at least not expressed openly. That can sometimes make the grieving process harder.

KATE

When Kate's mom died in an accident, some of the follow-up inquiries made it important that she kept her emotions in check. She said, "There were definitely limitations in how I've been able to grieve, just because there's ongoing legal stuff. My grief process started with a stage of anger because of her actions. When court things are ongoing, it's sometimes hard to be able to work through feelings of anger and move into other stages of grieving a loss."

DEXTER

When asked what he would share with a friend who was experiencing the death of a father, Dexter said that he'd say to expect bursts of anger along with other emotions. Dexter said, "From my experience, I'd say expect a lot of anger—just random weird anger. And it wouldn't necessarily be towards my dad for dying or toward somebody else for letting it happen, but just sadness and anger that seems to come out of nowhere." Playing video games was something Dexter used as an outlet for the anger he was feeling. He said that later he came to see that he was leaning too heavily on those games. "There were times I think I abused video games," he said, "and really got my anger going through those." But Dexter did come back around to see the value of letting the feelings of anger run through him and out of him in a healthier way, and to rely on others for support.

JDB

After JDB's dad died, he had plenty of feelings of anger about it, and not just toward people. "Angry?" JDB said, "Yes, I was angry. I went through a relapse with God and faith and all that. They say He's supposed to want the best for us. People would tell me, 'Oh, it's part of God's plan.' I'd think, 'Then why does the plan have to hurt me? It doesn't have to hurt me, does it?'"

It's not unusual for teenagers (or even adults or younger kids) to feel angry at the feelings of unfairness and injustice that their person died. It's not unusual for that anger to be expressed toward an idea of God or the cold world or an uncaring universe that took a loved one away from us, sometimes way too soon. It's okay to let yourself feel that anger. If it's in you, it's important to let yourself feel it and let it flow through you as part of the healing process. Explore it and even let it serve as a fire to keep you moving forward.

Like all the different feelings and phases of the grieving process, anger will come and go, mixed with other emotions. Recognize feelings of anger as coming from your pain and as a reflection of the depth of your love for your person who died. Letting yourself fully explore your feelings of anger can help you come to a broader understanding of your grief and help you find different perspectives on why you feel that anger.

BAILEY

Bailey has worked through some of those feelings of anger around her sister. "Those feelings of anger still come up," Bailey said. "I feel like it's okay to have these feelings as long as you know and understand that your person didn't die to hurt you, that wasn't what their intent was. They didn't control that; it just happened. But I feel like it's a bad thing to try and not feel those emotions. You should let yourself feel them."

KATE

As she has worked through her grieving process, Kate has been able to come to a better understanding of her mother's death and the effect it had on her and the rest of the family. She said, "At first I was angry with her actions. But when I really thought about everything she told me she went through in her life, I gained a better understanding of her own pain. I've tried hard to be self-reflective as I've gotten older. I work hard to be forgiving of my mother. But I am angry at the situation."

Feelings of anger are an expected part of the grieving process. Those feelings can carry you through. Anger may be part of the process because it's something you hold on to that's more solid than a sense of emptiness. Let yourself feel those emotions, and don't feel like you have to rush your way through them.

CHAPTER FOUR

GUILT AND REGRET

Guilt and regret are emotions that we're likely to feel when working through our process of grief. They're pretty closely related to anger. People sometimes even say that "guilt is anger being turned back in on ourselves." It's not uncommon to have feelings of guilt after the death of someone we love. Perhaps we feel like if we'd called our person to check in on them, maybe they wouldn't have taken their own life. If we hadn't hung out talking after school, maybe we would have gotten home twenty minutes earlier and been there in time to do CPR or call an ambulance. What if we'd pushed harder for our person to keep their doctor's appointments?

KATE

Kate said she felt like she had to resolve feelings of regret that she couldn't do more to help her mother through her addiction issues. "I wish I could have helped my mom more. I wish I could have changed things for her. In the aftermath, counseling helped me see that you can't change someone else's mind or change the way they act. I had to accept that I couldn't change how she was. The only thing you can change is yourself. That was a valuable lesson, and something I think that people sometimes forget."

BAILEY

Bailey spent time thinking about the idea of guilt after the death of her older sister. "When somebody you love takes their own life, it's important to remember that you didn't cause their death. Even

---

having said that, sometimes, I still blame myself for Sydney's dying. I think when something like this happens, there are going to be moments you look back and wish you would've played out something differently. 'What if I did this, or what if I said that?'"

Bailey was able to realize that it's normal for the mind to play with scenarios—different things you might have done that would have prevented your person from dying. In her grieving process, Bailey was able to see that letting the mind play with these scenarios can lead back to blaming ourselves for our person's death. "I think it's important to understand that it's okay to have regrets, and it's okay to wish things would've happened differently," she said. "But it's unfair to yourself to put the blame on your own shoulders."

If those feelings of guilt and regret do arise, they can crop up at unexpected times. Say, you might be at a party with your friends and catch yourself laughing at a joke or smiling at a story one of your friends is telling. You realize that you're smiling or laughing and then might feel guilty as if it might be disrespectful to the memory of your person if you're caught laughing.

Ask yourself if you should feel guilty about this thing. Ask yourself what your person would want for you. If you were to meet them down the road and they were to ask you, "Did you keep on playing practical jokes like we used to? How were the sunsets? Were they amazing? Did you find love?" If you responded that you stopped laughing and stopped watching sunsets and never let yourself love again because you would have felt guilty about that, what would your person say? Would they say that sounded like a good plan? Or would they want you to carry their memory forward into a life of meaning and joy? If you see them in a dream or a meditation, you might ask them.

If you find that feelings of guilt are creeping into your grief process, try being gentle and forgiving with yourself. Letting our minds get twisted around the axle of "If only . . ." won't help move us toward the healing we seek. Even if we had the power to go back in time, we could never be sure that changing a word or an action would make anything turn out differently than it did.

Like all the different stages of the grief process, it helps to let those experiences flow through you. Picture yourself holding those thoughts of "what if" in the palms of your hands. Examine them for what they are: simple regrets about things that are as they are. When you hold these thoughts and regrets in your palms and examine them for as long as you need, it will become easier to let go of them.

CHAPTER FIVE

BARGAINING

As part of the grieving process, "bargaining" can take many forms. If our person was suffering from cancer or some other lengthy illness, we may have engaged in bargaining while they were still alive. We may have called out quietly to the universe or to the God we believe in, with something that sounded like: "If you just heal my mom, I promise I'll never get into trouble again." Or "Please let my sister live just a little longer, and I'll give up my bad habits."

A wish like "Please let me wake up and have this all be a dream" can also be a form of bargaining. At the far end of the scale, bargaining might go as far as "I'll do anything if you bring my dad back to me." In bargaining, you can see how the emotions of grief can overlap and get mixed: the wish for "bring her back to me" is part bargaining and part denial, and "take me instead" could be bargaining and guilt all tangled together.

Bargaining is one of the ways we buffer ourselves against the pain of loss, and against the helplessness we feel about our person dying. It's a way we try to protect ourselves with an internal dialogue where we feel we might have some degree of control—in a circumstance where we feel overwhelmingly powerless.

JDB

Bargaining can appear in different degrees for different people. While most of our friends didn't recall having bargaining as a big part of the grieving process for them, JDB had put some thought into the topic. His opinions seem to reflect that he'd been able, with the help of his grief support group and counseling, to more

---

quickly come to a place of accepting the reality of his dad's death. "I don't really get the idea of bargaining," he said. "I don't have anything to bargain with. No amount of bargaining is going to bring him back, so why spend time thinking like that?"

It helps to recognize that bargaining is a normal part of the grieving process and helps by being a buffer between those stronger emotions that come up. Being able to recognize the thoughts of bargaining and negotiation for what they are can help you move through your process. Thoughts may still arise sometimes as you go forward, and you may find yourself wishing you could do something to change the present. But as you move forward, you'll probably find that those thoughts are less painful and less frequent. As you move to a place of accepting that your person has died and that no type of negotiation can change it, you may come to a place where thoughts of bargaining no longer serve you.

CHAPTER SIX
LONGING AND YEARNING

The feeling of yearning is probably what most people think of when they think about grief. Yearning is that acute sense of longing for a loved one who's no longer here, missing them, and feeling like we'd give anything to have them back in our lives. It may be hard to say whether any part of the grieving process is harder than another, but it can feel like the yearning is always present—even when we are also feeling the other emotions that go along with grieving. We can feel angry or disbelieving and still have a strong sense of longing to have our person back with us.

Longing is strong and ever present because the death of our person affects so many dimensions of who we are and how we exist in the world. We define ourselves, in part, by our relationships. You may have said to yourself that you "feel like a part of me is missing," or "I feel like there's a hole in here," or "It feels like a part of me died too." Does that sound familiar?

Maybe that thing you're describing is more than just a metaphor and is closer to the truth than you realize. If you're a daughter to your mother, who are you now after she has died? When your grandfather dies, and the two of you were best fishing buddies, who are you now after he has passed on? If your father dies, isn't that piece of you who is "a son" or "a daughter" missing too? Perhaps the feelings of intense longing we feel for our person who died is tied to us missing that part of ourselves and mourning the space inside of us that used to hold our person who died.

Another reason that yearning can feel so intense is that it comprises all the different dimensions of time: past, present, and future. We miss having them with us here now, and we also yearn for the experiences of our past with our person, the memories of which we only share with them.

KATE

Yearning for the past can take other forms too. Because Kate's mother had many addiction issues when Kate was a young teenager, she felt there were many parts of the mother-daughter relationship that she never got to experience. "A big part of my grief wasn't about the person I lost," Kate said, "it was the person I wish I would have gotten. I know that there's a version of my mother I will never get, the person I never got as a child. I didn't have a mother who was able to help guide me in growing up. It wasn't about just not having her here now or in the future. I felt the loss of not getting the person who, in my mind, I wanted when I was growing up." Kate felt her longing for her mother on other levels too. "I sometimes think about kids who knew their parent was dying. I envy that they had time to process things ahead of time and at least have some idea that 'this is going to happen.' For a long time, I felt angry that my future with my mom was no longer there for me, and those feelings could spin from yearning to anger to sadness and longing and back again. For me, it felt backward from how the normal grief process is supposed to go, whatever 'normal' is."

GRACE

The experience of yearning was an individual one for Grace. "I feel like my experience of longing was different from some of the other kids in my grief support group," Grace said. "I was four years old when my dad died, so a lot of my memories of him come from photos and videos, and Mom talking and telling stories about him. For a big part of my life, it wasn't like 'I had someone in my life who then left me.' It was more a feeling of missing a father who I never got to experience in my life in the first place."

Grace lost her father when she was young, but through group therapy she learned that there is hope, and things do get better. *Illustration by Kate Haberer*

The feeling of yearning in grief also has a "future element" to it. We've not only lost the person who is part of our memories from the past, and not just the person who we desperately wish was still here with us now, but we're also mourning the loss of the future we thought we would have with our person. We find ourselves having to let go of hopes and expectations and plans we'd had, sharing travels and adventures and explorations and all the other shared experiences we hoped we'd have with our person.

JDB

JDB reflected the father-son talks he'd had with his dad. "For most of my life, he was my best friend," JDB said. "We'd talk about all the things we wanted to do together. He really wanted to teach me how to drive. He talked about wanting to see me get married or graduate college—all that kind of stuff later down the road. The new *Star Wars* movie was coming out that year, and we were going to see it together because *Star Wars* was his favorite. It was coming out in December, but my dad died in November. . . . We didn't get to do anything on that list," JDB said. "When the *Star Wars* movie came out later, I went to see it by myself. I didn't like the movie that much, but it meant something and felt important because we had planned to see it together."

DEXTER

Dexter and his dad were movie fans too. His father had lined up a series of classic action films they were in the process of watching. "My dad was a big fan of the James Bond movies," Dexter said. "He told me, 'We're going to start with Sean Connery and go all the way through.' We were on Pierce Brosnan when he died. That's one thing I'm really going to miss. I just wish I could finish that whole movie series together with him."

KATE

Kate expressed a longing for the mother she hoped she might have had in the future. "I think about the person I'll never have as I get older," Kate said. "I won't have that mother to help me when I start dating someone. I'll never have that person who can talk me through when I'm sad or when I need a motherly figure to give me advice. I want to get married or have kids, and I'll miss not having her there to guide me."

You can embrace those feelings of longing and yearning. Some of the feelings and phases and emotions of your grieving process will lessen over time. Feelings of disbelief are likely to decrease as time goes on, and you begin to embrace the reality of what has happened. Even so, you may find yourself ten years down the road, still shaking your head and saying, "Ahh, I can't believe he's gone." Anger may lessen as you gain perspective on their death, and you find forgiveness for your person who died, or for others, or yourself.

Yearning and longing are harder, though, because those feelings carry all the warm memories and love and affection that still live on, even if your person is no longer physically here. You don't want to leave those memories and that love behind, but they can be so heavy and difficult to bear.

You might think of your yearnings and love and memories as if they were chunks of coal: in the fire, they can warm you, but they're dark, heavy, and so difficult to carry. You may not even know how to carry them. Do you put them in a backpack? Do you carry them in your bare hands, maybe the sharp edges cutting into your palms? Do you cram them into a burlap sack and drag them along behind you?

Regardless of how heavy they are, you wouldn't think of ever just leaving those pieces of coal behind you. No matter how much it hurts to carry them, they still represent your memories. Those heavy lumps of coal can transform. Look at the grieving process as something that provides heat and pressure. By letting the grief process do its work and letting yourself feel the emotions you need to feel to move forward, perhaps it is this pressure and heat that can transform a heavy and dark block of coal into a sparkling diamond of memory. By letting yourself experience your grief the way you need to experience it—with the help of your friends, family, grief groups, and counselors—you may find those heavy emotions of yearning change their form into something easier to carry.

It's the same chunk of mineral that it was before but now transformed into a jewel of memory that you can hold and turn in your hand, appreciating the sunlight hitting it at different angles. It's the same carbon, the same longing and yearning, only now lighter and brighter and easier to carry.

CHAPTER SEVEN

SADNESS AND COMPLICATED GRIEF

Feelings of deep sadness are a normal part of the grief journey. You'll feel sadness all along the path, and it's mixed in with all the other emotions you're experiencing at the moment (disbelief or anger or yearning or guilt). It's the most natural emotion in the world when you lose somebody so important in your life. The sadness is a protective buffer as you work to get your arms around the idea that your person is truly gone, and as you try to figure out what your relationship is going to be with your person as you go forward in your life. You can view sadness as the cushion you lean against as you redefine your sense of yourself in the absence of your person and find new ways of being in the world.

It helps to understand that these feelings of sadness and emptiness are normal responses in the grieving process. As with all the different phases and aspects of grieving, sadness is something that needs to keep flowing and moving, so things don't get stuck in place. Your grief happens in your own time, and you can be gentle and forgiving of yourself and take the time you need.

If you get to a place where you feel like you're stuck in place, you may be experiencing something they call "complicated grief." All grief is complicated, but when grief counselors talk about "complicated grief," they're referring to a person's experience where they aren't able to accept that their person is gone. Somebody who is experiencing complicated grief may have obsessive thoughts about their loss, or engage in ritualistic activities that interfere with daily life. Complicated grief may involve getting into unhealthy relationships, abusing substances, or avoiding new relationships in fear of losing someone again. Complicated grief can make you feel depressed and angry and make you feel like you're stuck there.

You might feel like you're powerless, or like you're trapped and have no end in sight for the pain of loss that you're feeling.

Kate felt that way sometimes. She said, "There were times I felt like I was in a box. Like I was restrained and couldn't escape." For JDB, his dad's death hit him hard, and there were points along the way that he felt almost immobilized by the intensity of his grief. "I was out of it for maybe six weeks," he said. "I was just a mess during that time. I missed school for about three weeks. For about two weeks, I cried spontaneously almost every day."

Remind yourself that you are not alone. You don't have to do this by yourself. If you need help finding a way around a spot in the path where you feel stuck, ask a school counselor, your family doctor, a grief counselor you're working with, or a trusted friend who's been down a similar path. Other people have walked a road like the one you're on. They have survived their losses and have been able to continue with lives of meaning and purpose—lives that honor their person who has died. You're not alone, and you can ask for help if you need it.

The Stoic philosopher Seneca, who lived in the first century, wrote a letter to his friend Marcia, who was still grieving hard after losing her son Metilius three years earlier. She must have been having complicated grief if three years had passed with no changes. In his letter, Seneca tries to counsel his friend, asking her if she would consider that her grief still had "lost none of its first poignancy, but renews and strengthens itself day by day, and has now dwelt so long with you that it has acquired a domicile in your mind." Seneca asks Marcia if she had considered that maybe her sadness had lingered so long that now it thought it had a right to stay there.

Seneca tells Marcia a story of two women similar to her: one who had stayed stuck and had buried herself in her grief; the other had chosen to honor her dead son, to put up his portrait in public places and speak of his memory with great pleasure. (One is grief and sadness remaining stuck, and the other is letting her grief move through her and expressing it in a healthy way.)

He finishes by inviting Marcia to "choose, therefore, which of these examples you think are more commendable." Seneca is saying we have a choice.

Have you ever seen the 2010 movie *Eat Pray Love* with Julia Roberts? The writer Elizabeth Gilbert authored the memoir that was turned into the film. During a 2019 speaking tour for her latest book *City of Girls*, Gilbert spoke openly about her personal experience of grief at the death by cancer of her partner Rayya Elias. In a web TV talk with host Marie Forleo, Gilbert had this to say about the relationship between depression and grief—and about the freedom to choose how to view grief and depression and loss. Gilbert told Forleo:

> Grief and depression are not the same thing. Depression is an inability to feel, a refusal to feel. It's a shutting down. Grief, when you allow it to live in its fire in you, is a very active, living force that has an element of rejoicing in it. And the rejoicing is to have loved so much that you are so devastated to have lost. That you *got* to love this much. It's very sacred.

It's a great way to think about sadness and grief, don't you think? Depressive feelings can help buffer and protect you while you adjust to the idea of your life going forward, a life where you're carrying your person with you in a different way than before. When deep sadness or depressive feelings have served their purpose, you have the freedom to choose to loosen your grip on them and let the current take them away. If those feelings overstay their welcome—like a party guest who won't leave when it's after midnight, and everyone else has gone home—you can ask for help in getting those feelings unstuck and showing them out the door. You can find a sense of power and control in knowing that you have a choice, like Gilbert said, of rejoicing that you were able to love this much. If you need help to find that power within you, all you need do is ask.

CHAPTER EIGHT

ACCEPTANCE AND GOING FORWARD

Acceptance is a part of the grieving process, and it's a stage that's often misunderstood. It's useful to start by looking at what acceptance is *not*. It's not "My best friend died, and I'm okay with it now." It's not the end of your sadness. It's not a destination or an endpoint. It's not a place where you're finally able to "put everything behind you." Acceptance doesn't mean that you're done feeling disbelief or yearning or anger. You'll still feel those emotions, but as you move forward, you may find they're less intense or happen less frequently.

JDB

JDB had some insights into how acceptance fit into his grieving process after his dad died. He said, "I think acceptance is not a place that you end up permanently. Even when you feel like you're at a place of acceptance, it's always going to be changing. You'll have lapses, and just feel the sadness come up at different times. It happened to me once on the anniversary of the day my dad died. I was minding my own business, maybe eating a sandwich or something. The sadness just came on, and I had this sudden feeling of being really small and insignificant. I've had four of those anniversaries now. Now, I try to treat those days like any other day, and take my comfort in remembering him."

After he lost his father, JDB felt all alone. However, after connecting with his father's friends and wearing his father's bracelets, he knew he was not alone and that he could keep his father's memory alive. *Illustration by Kate Haberer*

Acceptance starts to happen as you become better able to embrace the life you're given going forward. You're ready to accept that your person isn't here physically any longer. You're figuring out what your life will look like from here on out, and how you'll be able to redefine your relationship with your person who died. This is not how you would have chosen the story to go, but you're coming to embrace the new reality of it all. Acceptance can mean coming to a recognition that you are a different person now, going forward. You were a different person before, and now you are something new. Acceptance means figuring out how to put the pieces of ourselves back together in a way we can live with.

BAILEY

In her grieving process, Bailey was able to recognize and embrace a vision of what her life might look like after her sister died. She talked about redefining her idea of herself, and what normal was supposed to look like after the death of her sister. "Everything changed," Bailey said. "Normal wasn't normal anymore without her. After Sydney died, I felt like I had to relearn many aspects of my life and how to live without her."

DEXTER

Dexter talked about what it was like to gain some feeling of acceptance in the midst of the grief he was feeling. "After going through all the disbelief and the sorrow," he said, "you get to a place where you say, 'Okay, I'm trying to understand that this is the way it is.' I realized that I needed to help myself and resolve things in some kind of emotional way. I knew I needed to reconnect to my feelings in a healthy way."

Acceptance might be like a stretch of road where you have more good days than bad days. It might feel like a space that has a little more stability, a place where you start to spend more time feeling well than you do in yearning or despair. You begin to embrace the idea that while you'll always love and miss your person and have all the feelings of losing them, those feelings are something that you can bear. They're becoming memories that you feel you have the strength to carry.

Acceptance is being able to embrace that you're a new and different person now, never to be the one you were before. There can be strength and power in embracing that realization. In his novel *A Farewell to Arms*, Ernest Hemingway wrote: "The world breaks everyone, and afterward many are strong at the broken places." Embracing a sense of acceptance on your grief journey might be an example of the "strength at the broken places." So much of grief is feeling the powerlessness of losing someone you love so much, and feeling helpless to either bring them back or to go forward without them.

Part of acceptance is coming to a place where you're able to feel the broader and deeper truths of our lives: we all have set periods of time here. None of us knows how long we have. If we are to live fully and to embrace love, we'll inevitably feel the pain and grief of loss when people we love die—especially so if they die unexpectedly or in events that feel like they're outside of the natural order.

To the degree that we're able to embrace these realities of these human lives, there can come a sense of power, rather than helplessness. We can't change the way things are, but we can gain the power to understand how the world turns and that we can choose our thoughts. When someone you love dies, you will never be the person you were before. But the paths in front of you are rich with possibilities and vistas for you to continuing growing into the person you are becoming. Grief is a natural and inevitable counterpart to having loved deeply.

JDB

JDB talked about what he'd learned as he worked through the grief of his dad's death, and his feelings of acceptance around the realities of living and dying. He said, "I think death gets a bad rap sometimes. People think, 'It took someone away from me.' Well, yeah. But death also motivates everything. You can't live forever, and to be honest, that's probably what gets people out of bed in the morning, gets people doing things at the moment. I've learned you shouldn't procrastinate too much. I'll think, 'You know, three years from now could be my last. Or it could be tomorrow.' I just don't know, so why wait to do the important things?"

Embracing a feeling of acceptance also helped JDB gain some perspectives on how he'd grown and what he'd learned through his grief process. "There came a time when I came to terms with the idea that my dad had really died. It's hard to say things like, 'I'm sure there's a reason for it,' but I know I've met so many good people out of it so far. And I've been able to recognize how my dad impacted so many people, even though he had a shorter life span. Being able to accept his death has let me see some of those good things, too."

CHAPTER NINE

SEARCHING FOR MEANING

Have you looked at a fresh flower and a plastic flower and had an opinion on which one is more beautiful? Wouldn't you choose the fresh flower as more lovely, even if the plastic flower reflected the same colors? If the sun was always just below the horizon and the sky was always the same tapestry of crimson and orange and indigo, would sunsets become unremarkable, if not a little boring? The first snowfall in December always seems to have the air of magic that gets lost when the snow is still lingering in late January.

Part of what gives things their meaning and beauty is that we recognize that they're not permanent. A picked flower is fresh and fragrant only for a day or two before it begins to fade and wilt. The rich palette of a sunset will turn to gray as quickly as we look away. Snow melts.

In his letter of consolation to his friend Marcia, whose son had died, the Stoic philosopher Seneca reminds Marcia that life has meaning at all only because we die. He writes, "Life, it is thanks to Death that I hold thee so dear."

As we try to understand what grief is (disbelief, anger, bargaining, and the rest), it helps to know that "finding meaning" is an important part of the grief journey. Finding meaning in the death of a person you love—a parent or best friend or sibling—isn't about coming up with a reason. It's not anything like "they died as part of some greater plan" or anything like that. Finding meaning as part of your grief journey is more about what parts of your loved one you carry forward as you continue to live your life.

In his book *Finding Meaning: The Sixth Stage of Grief*, David Kessler writes beautifully and fills the pages with stories about the different ways that people have been able to find meaning in their lives after the death of someone they love. Meaning can be found in redefining how we look at what's happened to us. Instead of telling ourselves that our person's death was some kind of punishment or that we'll never be happy again, we can find meaning in being able to grow into the knowledge that their death was not our fault, or that it is possible to live with joy.

We can find meaning in how we carry our person's memory forward in our lives, and that we show ourselves that it's possible to live with more happiness than pain, even though we'll always miss them. We can live in a way that honors the life of our person as we go forward, not destroyed and broken but living a fulfilling and purposeful life.

Kessler tells a story about visiting Hamburg, Germany, and coming across the Church of St. Nikolai, which was completed in the year 1195. During World War II, when much of Hamburg was destroyed by Allied bombing, the church tower and some of the walls of St. Nikolai remained standing. After the war, much of the city was rebuilt. The remnants of St. Nikolai were left to stand as they were. Gardens and sculptures were added on the grounds as a memorial to what had happened there.

Kessler reflects on Hamburg's Church of St. Nikolai as an example of how to live with meaning: honoring the pain of devastation and loss, while building a beautiful life and a new city around it.

PART II

COPING WITH GRIEF

As you search for different ideas about how you might work with your grief, it should help to remind yourself again that you're not alone on this road. You don't have to figure everything out for yourself. Many teens have walked this path before you, and they have lots of ideas to share. Our friends Kate, Bailey, Dexter, Logan, JDB, and Grace have all lost people in their lives too. They've tried many different things as they've worked their way through their grieving processes. They've had lots of help from other teens, adults, and professionals. They didn't do it alone, and you don't have to either.

It's been said that "there are the things that happen to us," and then "there are the ways we think about those things." You certainly can't turn off your thoughts and feelings, nor would you want to; those thoughts are part of the treasured legacy of your person, which you'll carry with you in your life going forward. You can't think your way out of your grief or talk yourself out of your feelings, but you can choose how to think about the pain you're experiencing.

Our friends offer suggestions about how they've coped and how they work through the process of grieving their person. They'll talk about different practices they've tried that have helped them care for their minds and their bodies and their spirits. They'll share some of their insights about ways they've reached out for help, whether that be through support groups or finding the right counselor they could trust.

They'll share their thoughts about what's been challenging in relating to friends and others in the aftermath of the death of their person, and ways they've found to respond when friends or family or acquaintances have a hard time understanding what they're going through. You'll hear them share observations on what has worked well for them, and approaches they feel didn't serve them so well.

We've said that there's no single way to go through the grieving process. Some things work well for one person, and some things work better for another. Hopefully, you'll feel some sense of reassurance and control in this—especially when so many other things feel like they're out of your control.

None of our friends have found that the same thing works for all of them. You might relate more to Bailey or Kate, who found that talking with counselors helped them more than being with other teens in a support group. On the other hand, Logan and Grace both found great value in being able to talk with other teens who'd experienced the death of someone close.

Journaling or just writing out thoughts and observations about life has been helpful to JDB, but Bailey never found much use for writing about her feelings.

The voices of our friends in the following pages are evidence that you can find lots of different ways to approach grief and work through your feelings after the death of someone you love. There's no single best way to do it, and that might give you a sense of strength—that you can decide for yourself what is helpful to you.

CHAPTER TEN

TAKING CARE OF YOUR MIND AND SPIRIT

Feelings of grief can be so vast and overwhelming, and you may sometimes think that you can't carry that burden. The good news is that you don't have to carry all that hurt and pain. British movies portray the value of "keeping a stiff upper lip." Old Westerns show us "the strong, silent type" as some kind of ideal. Keeping one's feelings about grief bottled up isn't the best approach.

A couple of sayings kept coming up when our friends would talk about their experiences of grieving their loved ones. They'd say things like: "You have to feel it if you want to heal it." Another one was: "The only way around the grief is to go through it." All that heaviness and hurt and feelings of yearning can't just sit inside of you. Those feelings need to go somewhere, so there can be room inside you for the other emotions that need to come next.

One of the important ways to move forward with the grieving process is to let yourself feel those emotions and let them flow through you. It's a natural part of the process of moving through grief: it can give you a feeling of release and cleansing, and make room for more positive energy. Writers who study their fellow humans have recognized the benefit of this emotional release. You can look back to Shakespeare in his play *King Henry VI*, where he wrote: "To weep is to make less the depth of grief." Letting yourself have a good cry can help ease some of the pain of loss.

The value of letting your feelings flow through you hasn't been lost on modern writers either. Anne Lamott, who wrote *Bird by Bird*, a great book about the writing process, talks about losing people we love, handling grief, and what we can gain by giving ourselves a good cry. In her 2017 TED Talk "12 Truths I Learned from Life and Writing," Lamott says of the loved ones we lose:

> Their absence will also be a lifelong nightmare of homesickness for you. Grief and friends, time, and tears will heal you to some extent. Tears will bathe and baptize and hydrate and moisturize you and the ground on which you walk.

Isn't that a great way to think of it? Giving yourself time and letting the tears flow will heal you "to some extent." It won't make everything okay and won't make the pain stop, but it can help. In her 2016 novel *LaRose*, Louise Erdrich writes about the eight-year-old Ojibwe boy LaRose, who is at a family gathering where the spirits of their ancestors are gathered around, whom only he and the dog can see. The spirits of their ancestors are speaking to him in both English and Ojibwe:

> They sat on chairs made of air and fanned their faces with transparent leaves. They spoke in both languages. We love you. Don't cry. Sorrow eats time. Be patient. Time eats sorrow.

Though we've already decided that crying is okay (sorry, Louise and Ojibwe spirits), those spirit words about patience and time resonate with what Lamott was saying. You can be gentle and patient with yourself because time will eat some of your sorrow for you.

Letting your feelings flow and not letting them get stuck is important for more emotions than just sadness.

KATE

Kate talked about the full spectrum of emotions she felt after her mom died, and how important she thought it was to let herself experience all those feelings. "Everyone has their feelings of guilt or sadness or anger," Kate said. "I think that if you want to move forward, you have to let yourself feel those feelings. Let yourself accept them and then let go of them if you can. When I've been able to talk about my personal experiences or things that have happened in my life, it feels like a weight's been lifted off me. Sometimes I feel like a lot of humanity doesn't do that. If we did, maybe we would feel better about a lot of things."

Letting yourself experience the sharp yearning or dull, throbbing loneliness of missing your person can be hard, and it's not the same for everyone. Especially if we've been brought up in an environment that says, "Crying equals weakness" or "Being the strong silent type equals strength."

LOGAN

Logan found it a real balancing act for him, feeling like he had to meet the needs of his family members while still taking care of himself. He said, "My dad was one for bottling up your emotions. I took on that mind-set, and it made me feel like I had to be strong for my little brother Jake and Mom. But at the right time and the right spot, I felt like I could deal with my emotions and let them show. I got to the point where I think I showed my brother that being vulnerable was okay. Sometimes you have to keep your feelings to yourself, but then let yourself feel them later. It has to be up to you, on your own time scale," Logan said.

GRACE

Grace has had a long time to learn to work with her feelings of loss and let them flow through her. As a thirteen-year-old whose dad died when she was four, Grace has been without her dad twice as long as she had him in her life. For most of her life, she's been trying to learn how time and understanding can move her toward feeling whole. "It's hard work to feel your feelings, and it just takes time," Grace said. "It feels like part of you is gone, because your person who died was a huge part of you. It's a wound, and like all wounds, things have to heal. Parts of you have to heal, and you have to pay attention to that. Over time and as you grow, you can start to understand better how you've dealt with it up to now and how you can deal with it in the future. I tell other kids that over time, it does get better."

BAILEY

It's been hard for Bailey since her sister died. She's grown in her awareness of how her emotions can rise and fall, and how important it's been for her to let herself experience what she's feeling. "There are always going to be lows," Bailey said. "Even as time passes, I don't think you can avoid those lows. There will always be something that will trigger those feelings that make you realize how much you miss the person that you lost. You're going to feel all that pain and grief like it's a brand-new pain. This isn't something you can avoid. So I've learned that it's important to embrace those feelings and let yourself experience them when they come. It helps to get those feelings out—instead of holding them inside."

Letting yourself feel the sadness, letting it run through you, can help keep that sadness moving to make space for some happiness to come in. If you try to hold back the sadness, you'll also be blocking that happiness that is waiting to fill that space. Jonathan Safran Foer's novel *Extremely Loud and Incredibly Close* (which is also an Oscar-nominated movie with Tom Hanks and Sandra Bullock) tells the story about Oskar, a boy whose father died in the World Trade Center on 9/11. A friend is trying to tell Oskar that it's okay to let himself feel his pain, to let it flow through him. His friend tells Oskar, "You cannot protect yourself from sadness without protecting yourself from happiness."

MEDITATING

Meditation is a practice that has been helping people work with their thoughts for thousands of years. You can find seven-thousand-year-old sculptures from India that show people who are sitting and meditating. Written records from thirty-five hundred years ago talk about the practice of "training your mind." What is meditation, and is it something that you could try as a way of working with everything you're feeling with the death of your person? We've talked about how it can help to let your thoughts and feelings flow through you, and meditation might be a practice that can help you do that.

We can start by saying what meditation is *not*. Many people think that meditation is something you do to "clear your mind." Meditation is not about stopping your thoughts—nobody can do that. Meditation is about learning to observe your thoughts and being able to have the awareness that you have thoughts, but you are not your thoughts. A meditation instructor asked the students in her class to hold up their thumbs. She asked them a question: "Look at your thumb and ask yourself, 'Am I my thumb? Or do I have a thumb?'" Everyone in the class answered, "I have a thumb, but this thumb is not 'me.'" You can think of your "thoughts" as your "thumb" in this example.

Meditation is a practice that can help give a person a healthy perspective and the awareness that "I have thoughts, but I am not my thoughts." Meditation can give you the power to observe, without becoming attached. Instead of "I *am* angry" or "I *am* missing my brother," would it help to be able to say, "There's a thought; it looks like anger," or "I'm observing the feeling of missing my brother." You are not becoming angry or sad, but you can observe those thoughts and feelings in your mind.

There's a release, a freedom that can come with being able to observe your thoughts as they arise, and as they pass—to be able to notice them without judgment. During the grieving process, when feeling overwhelmed with thoughts of yearning and anger, despair and helplessness, or guilt and regret, it can help to be able to step back and gain the awareness that these are thoughts you're having, but those thoughts are not you. The thoughts don't need to control you.

You'll hear people talk about different styles of meditation: transcendental meditation or TM, mindfulness meditation, or loving-kindness meditation. Yoga is a form of meditation. There are different practices that people follow when they meditate: they might repeat a word or "mantra," or they might focus their attention on an image or the feeling of their breath. Here's how simple meditation can be, in three steps:

1. Get comfortable, with your eyes closed and your back straight.
2. Be aware of the feeling and sensation of your breath: the air passing through your nostrils and chest and your belly rising and falling.
3. As you put your awareness on the sensation of your breath, you'll start to notice thoughts coming up. That's okay. It's part of how this works. When thoughts arise, bring your awareness back to your breath—and begin again.

That's it. Let's see what this might look like in practice. Start by getting comfortable. You can sit on the floor, sit on a pillow, sit in a chair, or sit outside under a tree—with your back straight. You can lie down if you want, but sometimes that makes it a little too easy to fall asleep. You want to be relaxed but aware. If you find yourself snoozing off, try sitting up with your back straight. No special positions are required—you don't have to twist your legs into a pretzel or stand on your head. Just sit straight and comfortably and close your eyes.

Now put your attention on the feelings of your breath coming in and out of your body. You're not "thinking about your breath," but just noticing the sensation. Inhale and notice the coolness of the air coming in through your nostrils, or the sense of your chest and belly expanding. On the exhale, feel the falling of your belly, the contraction of your chest, or the warmth of the air passing out of your nostrils. In and out. Rising and falling. You're not "having thoughts about breathing"—but simply putting your awareness on the sensations of your breath.

Something funny happens when you bring your mind's focus onto the feeling of your breath: your mind starts to chatter away. Thoughts start getting noisy and competing for that quiet space you're creating for yourself. Those thoughts can be anything:

- "Uh-oh. I'm supposed to clear my mind. I must not be doing this right."

- "I should be doing homework. I'm supposed to read chapter 16 before class tomorrow."

- "I wonder what's for dinner."

- "You know what would make a great Instagram post?"

- "I should be doing something else now."

- "I miss my dad."

Buddhists call this "monkey mind," and it's a good metaphor. Thoughts are swinging from branches, yammering wildly, throwing bananas at your other thoughts. When people try to meditate for the first time and experience that jabbering monkey mind, they figure, "Nope. I guess I can't do it. I can't clear my mind. *My* mind is just too busy. I guess meditation isn't for me." People who try meditation—teenagers included—often stop at this point. They figure that since they can't "clear their mind," meditation must be a trick that only special people can do. They quit and go watch Netflix or check their phones.

Here's the secret: that very moment of recognizing that your attention is on a thought and no longer on your breath, that is the little victory you're looking for—that pure awareness. No fault. No judgment. All you do is bring your attention back to the sensation of your breath, and you begin again. Like every person who's ever practiced meditation for the past seven thousand years, your mind will get distracted by another thought. You will notice it and bring your attention back to your breath. You will begin again and again.

We mentioned that one way meditation can help is by giving you a different and healthy perspective. This simple meditation exercise gives you that "different perspective." Instead of "My mind wandered; I failed," your perspective can be, "I noticed a thought and brought my mind back to my breath. I succeeded."

Here's another way that people sometimes imagine this process of training your attention: picture yourself sitting on a cushion along the bank of a slow-moving river. The sun is shining, and you're in the shade of a large oak tree. You're feeling the sensations of your breath going in and out, your chest and belly rising and falling. The waters of the river flow past you. The water is not in any hurry. It's just flowing. As your eyes rest gently on the current, you notice a single leaf drifting past on the water's surface.

You could jump up and splash into the water, grab the leaf, and bring it back to shore. You could shake the water off it, turn it over in your hands, and try to decide if it's a maple leaf or a sycamore leaf. You could take a picture and post it to Instagram with the caption "I plucked this random leaf out of the river. #naturelover #meditationexpert."

Or, you could sit quietly on the riverbank in the speckled shade of that oak tree, and simply be aware of the leaf without attaching yourself to it. Notice how it arrived on the current, all on its own. You can name it. It's a leaf. Perhaps you make a note of its shape and whether it's fresh and green, or withered and brown. Then watch how the current carries the leaf away and out of your sight, without any effort from you. Then you bring your attention back to the feelings of your breath and begin again. Does it feel like a small victory to recognize that you were able to notice: "Ahh. There's a leaf. My breath goes in; my breath goes out"?

Plenty of evidence is out there about what meditation can do for people. It can help with negative emotions. One study showed that a practice of meditation could reduce anxiety and depression at a level that rivaled antidepressant medications. Meditation can help improve sleep, and it can give people skills they can use to manage stress and gain new perspectives. With MRI scanners, they can show that meditation quiets activity in the part of the brain that's responsible for that "monkey mind" chatter and strengthens parts of the brain that help with emotional regulation. ABC News journalist and meditator Dan Harris says that meditation "is like doing a bicep curl for your brain."

Letting meditation help you find new perspectives and being able to observe your thoughts can help as you go through your grieving process. For example, it can help you recognize that there's a difference between pain and suffering. You can think of "pain" as the signal that tells you something hurtful is happening to you. "Suffering," though, is your mind's interpretation as it struggles to make some kind of sense and meaning out of that pain. They say that pain is something we work through, but the suffering part is optional.

Meditation can help in figuring out how to approach that suffering. It can help you recognize that thoughts and emotions will rise of their own accord, and if you don't attach yourself to them, they will drift away of their own accord too. It can help you recognize that what is truly "you" is not "your thoughts." What is truly "you" is the awareness that sits behind the thoughts and observes the thoughts. By observing, you can bring your attention back to your breath and begin again. Each time you begin again is one more step along the path of healing.

Author and former Buddhist monk Jack Kornfield has talked about the insights into grief that we can gain from a practice of meditation:

> What I know from fifty years of meditation and doing hospice work is that we are not just this body. You are made of spirit. And the spirit makes it so that even if people have died, we're still profoundly connected to them in love. In that sense, they haven't exactly died. They are in us, not only in our hearts but also somehow in our very being. Knowing this does not take the grief away, and it doesn't take away the power of that grief to shake us to our roots, but it lets us know something bigger than all of that: Who I am is not just this body. We are consciousness.

Our friends have tried different types of meditation, and have found things that worked for them.

KATE

Kate said, "There's this great app that my therapist gave me called Breathe2Relax. If I'm super stressed and pent up, it helps me settle down and focus. It gives you this calming music, and it guides you through an exercise of inhaling and then exhaling. I feel like it decompresses me and makes me feel more open. When I feel fully open, it feels like I'm going on a spiritual journey where I can let it go, and can take on the world. It gives me time for self-reflection. It feels like one of the most important things we can do."

DEXTER

Dexter said that once he learned about yoga and meditation, he wished he'd started practicing it earlier. "Now I try to do at least five or ten minutes of some kind of yoga or meditation every day," he said. "During the day, I set a reminder on my watch to stop and just breathe for five minutes. I'll also do a breathing exercise if I'm having some kind of stressful moment. After I do it, I feel ten times better. It absolutely provides me with clarity about the things I'm facing with this body and with my surroundings."

The resources section in this book lists some meditation resources and apps that many people find valuable. Headspace, Waking Up, Calm, 10% Happier, and Breathe2Relax are some widely used apps. Most of these apps have basic free guided meditations, free trial periods, and subscription offerings. You can also go to YouTube and search for "guided meditations" or "meditation for beginners" and find some good videos you can try. The bibliography also lists a couple of good books on meditation by a Buddhist nun named Pema Chödrön.

In one of the sessions in Sam Harris's Waking Up meditation app, Harris talks about the practice of meditation. He says, "I assure you that if you continue with it, you will find something of real interest here. After all, you really only have your mind. It's the basis of everything you experience. It is *you* in each moment, and to understand it deeply—not as a matter of theory, but directly—to recognize how consciousness is, prior to thinking or reacting or trying to change your experience in any way at all, can be the most important thing you ever learn to do."

Keep in mind that when you meditate, you have nowhere to go. You have nothing to do. Everything you need is already inside you.

PRAYING

You may count yourself as a follower of a religion, or you may not. You may think of yourself as a Jew, a Buddhist, a Muslim, a Catholic, or a Hindu. You may have grown up Sikh, Jain, Shinto, Christian, pagan, or any of the forty-two hundred religions that are practiced around the world. You may consider yourself an agnostic. You may be an atheist and feel that there is no God. Wherever you stand, it's all right. There's no evangelizing here.

Whether you believe in a God or you don't, praying is something you may find helpful as you work with your grief. If you are part of a wisdom tradition that has ceremonies, ministers, and revered books that carry special prayers or words of comfort or insight, you can lean on those things, for sure.

Even if you don't feel part of those traditions, you can still find some comfort in praying. Maybe it would help to talk a minute about what we mean when we talk about "prayer." In his book *Healing Words: The Power of Prayer and the Practice of Medicine*, Dr. Larry Dossey writes about the word "prayer" coming from the Latin root *precari*: "to ask earnestly." He talks about two kinds of prayer: one form being a petition (where the person is asking something for oneself), and the other as intercession (where a person is asking something for others).

Whether for yourself or another person, prayer can be pretty straightforward: it's as simple as having a compassionate and loving thought for another person and asking for well-being or peace or understanding. That's it. Dr. Dossey says that it doesn't matter how long your prayer lasts, or what words you use. What matters, he says, is the intensity and genuineness and authenticity of the love that the praying person has.

Prayer doesn't need to be words, although you can recite something if you want—say, an invocation from your traditions, a poem, or song lyrics. Another way to pray might be to visualize what "well-being" might look like for you: a ray of sunshine entering your chest, colored confetti drifting down around you, or a warm summer breeze lapping across your skin like a wave.

Praying for other people, or "intercessory prayer," is something that may benefit you, too. Intercessory prayer can be you sending a message of love to your person who died. Praying for someone else can look like you directing some of that sunlight or those warm breezes through you and toward them. You could hold in mind any suffering person as the object of your prayer—you don't even have to know their name.

How can it help you to send prayers or good thoughts or bright images to other people when *you're* the one who's grieving? It's hard to say how, but for some reason, it does help. Maybe it's because your intent to be an instrument of healing to another person also makes you a conduit for love. There's a saying in the Jewish Talmud that's been translated as: "Whoever saves a single life, it is as if they have saved an entire world." If we're all one thing, perhaps when we channel love and kindness to another suffering person through prayer, that act of generosity helps make them whole, and in that act helps heal us all—including yourself.

Does it matter "who" you're praying to? If prayer is a message, does it matter whose name is on the envelope, be it Yahweh, Allah, Jah, Jesus, or Zeus? If you have a wisdom tradition or religion that makes sense to you, you probably don't need help answering that question. If you're not sure about religion or undecided on your ideas about God, maybe it doesn't need to matter so much.

In her *Super Soul Conversations* podcast, Oprah Winfrey talked with religious scholar Karen Armstrong, a former Catholic nun and author of more than two dozen books on world religions. Winfrey asked Armstrong, "What is your definition of God?" Even after she had studied and written about God and religion for more than thirty years, Karen's answer went like this:

> I refuse to define God. God cannot be defined because the word "define" means "to set limits on something." God is more than we can conceive. As the Muslims say, "Allahu Akbar," which means "God is always greater," greater than we can imagine or think. There are no words [that can contain God]. It's like the end of a symphony when the last notes die away, and there's a pregnant beat of silence in the hall before the applause begins. And when we talk about God, we're supposed to lead people into that beat of silence, where you say, "Ahh, that's it. Nothing to be said."

If there is something bigger than ourselves, something that knits us all together and responds to our intent for love and healing for each other, does it matter what we call it? Armstrong says that she can see that thing in the eyes of an animal, other people, and the world around us.

WRITING

JOURNALING

Holding lots of strong emotions inside of you can be stressful. Giving yourself the freedom to express some of those thoughts and emotions in a private journal—to empty those emotions onto a page—can help relieve some of that stress. Journaling can give you a private place to explore and discover what's going on inside of you. A journal can help by giving you a record of where you've been, give you something to return to and review as a record of your journey, and help you identify recurring topics on which to focus.

You can write about painful memories or regrets. Write about the good memories or favorite vacations or trips you took with your person.

If there are things you wish you would have talked about with them, you can write about it in your journal. If you feel angry about something they did or didn't do, your journal is a good place to get that out—to give it a place to live besides letting it live inside of you. Getting your feeling out on the page, and into the light, can make room for new thoughts and feelings inside of you.

Your journal can be a place where you make notes about things you want to talk about with a counselor, or with other teens in your grief support group. You can keep track of how you're sleeping, what your mood is like, or your appetite. Have you been working out or riding your bike or going for runs in the woods? A journal is a good place to write down how you were feeling before your bike ride and after. That journal entry might be the thing that gives you a little nugget of practical self-advice: "You know, I can see from my journal that every time I go for a trail run, I always seem to feel better." Writing in your journal can help with these moments of self-discovery.

Your private journal is just for you. You can be more open with yourself if you make sure it stays private. When you know you're the only one who will see what you're writing, you can be more open and honest with yourself about how you're feeling, even if those feelings are dark or raw. If you feel like somebody might read your stuff, it might make you feel restrained and make you hold back from writing the things you think or feel—which is the very honesty that will help you the most.

In a private journal, you can let your thoughts pour out of you. If you feel like crying while you're writing in your journal, you can cry. If you remember goofy things your person used to say or do, you can write about that and laugh as you're remembering—without feeling like you'll be judged for laughing. If you're feeling angry or depressed, you can be honest on the page if you know this journal is for "your eyes only."

Just like everything else in the grieving process, there's no one-size-fits-all approach to journaling. Our friends have all had different experiences with the practice of writing in a journal. Bailey never thought journaling was helpful to her and said she's never written in a journal about her feelings. Our other friends have found journaling to be useful in different ways.

DEXTER

Dexter was able to use his journal as a tool to help him understand when something was bothering him but wasn't quite sure what that thing was. He said, "If I'm feeling particularly stressed out or I'm just not feeling my best, I'll write down some of the things I'm thinking. I'll try to sort out 'Okay, what's making me not feel good? How can I address this and release it in a positive way without harming myself or others around me?'"

KATE

Kate said that, for a time, she journaled a lot. It helped her get feelings out and be honest with herself about how things were going for her. "When I write, I'm able to open myself up," she said. Kate also recognized how important it was for her to keep her journals private.

"When I was dealing with some depression, some of my thoughts were not great, and it was a scary place for me," Kate said. "Writing was an outlet for me to go through those thoughts and figure out what I needed to do to help myself. When I'm writing about things like that, I don't intend for anyone else to read it. I had to change my approach after my sisters found one of my journals and read it. Of course, it was upsetting to them. I told them I understand that people are curious to know what's going on in someone else's mind, but that they shouldn't be reading someone else's private journal." Kate changed her journaling approach for a while. She found that it was still helpful to her to write out her honest thoughts and feelings, and then to delete what she wrote. "It helps me to feel it, to write it, and then get rid of it," she said. "It's a way I can get my feelings out and still keep my own autonomy."

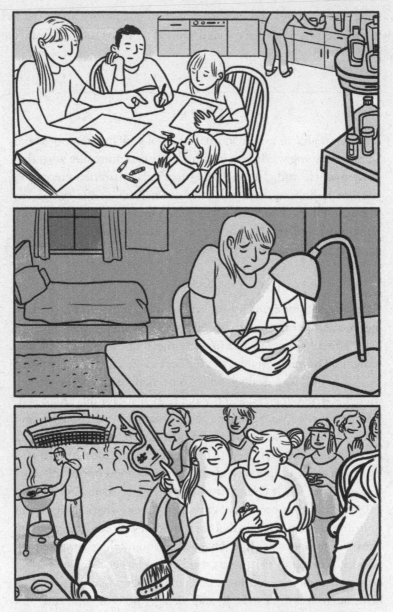

Due to her mother's addictions, Kate was often caretaker for her siblings. After her mother died, Kate would write about her feelings in her private journal, helping her come to terms with her feelings and find a way forward through her grief. *Illustration by Kate Haberer*

JDB

JDB doesn't write in his journal all the time, but when he does, he finds it's been helpful to him. He tries to take a broader perspective on the topics he writes about and doesn't just focus on feelings about the death of his dad. "I would say this about writing in journals: don't limit yourself to just writing about your grief," he said. "Having my dad die was huge, and it's hard to keep that one event from consuming your whole life. I've seen it sometimes happen with other kids, and it's kind of scary to see how someone can stay down in the dumps for years on end. You have a life to live, too. It's true that you can't rush things, so you have to give it time. Journaling can help you see that you can get through it."

Here are some ideas and tips if you want to try journaling:

- You don't need anything fancy, just a notebook and a pen, or a document on your computer.

- Remind yourself that what your writing is only for you. If your journal is on your computer, you could put a password on the file to make you feel confident that your journal will stay private.

- Make a date with yourself to write every day at the same time. It doesn't have to be long; ten or fifteen minutes is good. You might find yourself going longer, but if you get in the routine of saying: "I'm going to journal for ten minutes at 7:00 a.m. every morning," you'll be more likely to do it.

- When you sit down, just start writing, and keep your pen moving (or keep your keyboard clicking). You don't have to have a plan. You can start with something as simple as: "I told myself I'd journal for twenty minutes, but I have no clue what I want to say. I miss my mom. This is stupid, and I'd rather be outside walking the dog. That reminds me of a time when . . ." Just keep your pen moving, and you may be surprised by the direction your thoughts take you.

- Don't worry about spelling or grammar or finding the exact right word. Make it messy; make it sloppy. Leave out all the commas or put commas after every word. Who cares? This is just for you, and nobody else is going to see it. You'll find that your thoughts will start flowing onto the page more quickly if you don't stop to edit yourself. Just slap your paint on the canvas.

- Write whatever you want. If you hit on a topic that makes you shiver or want to cry or want to yell out, stay with it. That's where the power is.

You can hit the page running and see where your thoughts take you. Sometimes it's also good to start with a writing prompt and explore your thoughts that way. Some writing prompts might include:

- A good memory of your person

- The bravest thing you ever saw them do

- Something you're mad about

- Something you said that you wish you could take back

- Something you're doing that you think would make them proud of you

If you pour your feelings and thoughts, anger and fear, hopes and joys, your longing and sadness into your journal, it can end up being your confidant, your confessor, or your wilderness guide. Your journal can help you read the map of where you've been, how you got to where you are now, and where you're going.

WRITING STORIES

Your journals are for yourself. Writing fictional stories to share with others can be another way that writing can help you work through the grieving process. As with your journals, you can choose to write these stories for yourself or to share with other people. Stories can help uncover, build understanding, connect the pieces, and help throw light and hope on things that would otherwise be dark or hopeless. Sharing our stories can help us all feel less alone.

You may have read John Green's best-selling novel *The Fault in Our Stars*, a story about two teens going through their own experiences of cancer. Green talks about the power of writing fiction to help us deal with suffering and loss. He says: "I believe there's hope for us, even amid the suffering. And that's why I write fiction, probably. It's my attempt to keep that fragile strand of radical hope, to build a fire in the darkness."

Writing stories is a way we can build a fire for ourselves, and maybe illuminate some of the dark corners where pain and unexamined thoughts may be hiding. Writing stories can be one way to let emotions flow through us. They can help us imagine other story lines in our own lives. They can help us envision what our potential futures might look like—and take those futures for a test-drive to see how they handle, how they corner, how the wheel feels in our hands.

We connect with other people through stories. They're one way that we're able to share the deepest parts of ourselves—like Green said about building a fire in the darkness, our most ancient experience of sharing stories most likely happened around a fire tens of thousands of years ago. The storyteller held the rapt attention of others in her tribe and spun her tales as her people leaned in close: gasping at the surprises, laughing at the humor, and crying through the tragedies. The experience of sharing stories spreads the emotion, lets the people we're telling the story carry some of that emotion with us, and helps bond us to each other.

If you write your stories as fiction, it can give you a buffer between the rawness of the reality you're feeling against what you work out in a made-up story. If you tell a fiction story about "this girl Mandy and her mom named Linda," rather than a true story about "me and my mom," it gives you some room to play with a character's experiences and see things from a different perspective. It can help you see things through different eyes, to sort out your feelings, or just to connect with your departed person in the space of the made-up story.

If you write a story as fiction, you have more freedom to be creative in working out the ideas in your mind. Here are a couple of prompts for fictional story ideas that may help as you're working through your grieving process:

- A son and his father go for a backpack in the mountains, lose track of each other, and try to find one another.

- A girl and her best friend spend almost every summer day together at the pool, going to movies, and hanging out with friends. The girl learns that her best friend is moving to another state.

- A brother and sister discover that their mother is quite ill, and talk about plans for a future where they don't know what will happen next.

KATE

Writing a story where you have fictional characters who are surrogates for you or other people in your life can be a creative way to experiment with your feelings and let things play out in different ways. Kate said she does this sometimes. She said, "I daydream a lot. I like to come up with different stories and ways of figuring things out by telling them in my own personal way. I like that a lot."

WRITING ESSAYS

Essays are another form of writing. Journaling is usually a private exercise for your eyes only, and fiction is a more creative process of making up stories. Essays or memoirs are a form of nonfiction writing where you're telling your real-life story as you want to tell it. You can share your essays with other people, or you can write them and keep them private if you wish.

Essays or memoirs are a good way to share the hurt and the hopes you feel, the regrets or longing, or the memories you have of your person. You can tell the story of how your person died, stories of special times together, or what your journey of grief has been like for you. If you choose to share your essays with other people, they can be a good way for you to help them understand what you're going through on your journey, which might be harder to share if you were sitting across the table from them.

Suppose you wrote an essay about how your phone has a special ringtone for your best friend who died last year. Your essay could talk about your memories, the pain, or the warm and happy reflections that come up in your mind whenever you hear that ring. When you write that essay and get those thoughts onto the page, it can help you to crystallize those memories, so you can come back and reflect on them later.

Writing essays could also be useful to other teens who are walking the same path as you. They may read your essay and think, "That same thing happens to me when I hear my sister's ringtone." It may make them feel less alone, knowing that other teens like you are going through the same kinds of experiences as they are.

If you want to share the essays that you write, a personal blog is an excellent way to do that. Platforms like Blogger or WordPress are free and easy to set up. Another idea is to submit your essays to sites like the Grief Dialogues or AfterTalk or share them in grief forums (with some ideas listed in the resources section at the back of this book).

WRITING A LETTER TO YOUR PERSON

Some teens find that it helps them work through their feelings of grief by writing a letter to their person who died. Although it may seem like a one-sided conversation, it's one way to stay connected to them. You can write to them and tell them about how much you miss them, or about something you did yesterday that made you think of them. Your letter to them doesn't even have to be about your feelings about missing them. You can have your side of the conversation and tell them about making the cut for your high school volleyball team, the date you had last weekend, or how much you like the latest program you're binge-watching on Netflix.

Maybe you feel a sense of relief for your person because they were suffering before, and now they're not. In your letter, you can tell them you're relieved for them. Write as if they'll be reading your words. Write as if they can hear you. What can it hurt? Tell them how you've visited their gravesite, and maybe about the memento you left for them on your last visit. Tell them about how you did on your school finals last week, or how it always made you feel less anxious when the two of you studied together. Do you feel regret about that last fight you had and wish that you could take back something harsh that you said? A letter to them is a good way to be able to tell your person the things you want to say to them.

You can send a text, write a letter on nice stationery, or send an email. Tell your sister you miss her. Tell your dad you love him. You can use your letter or email to tell them good-bye and that you'll see them again.

You might be familiar with novelist Tim O'Brien. Many high school English classes study his 1990 book *The Things They Carried*. In his more recent *Dad's Maybe Book*, O'Brien works with this idea of letters you send across time, between people who may not be on this earth at the same time. O'Brien was in his late fifties when he and his wife, Meredith, had their sons, Tad and Timmy. O'Brien did the math and figured he'd be in his seventies by the time his boys started driving, dating, or shaving. By the time they became young men, he was going to be an old man. He'd likely be mistaken for their grandfather instead of their father.

When the boys were still little kids, O'Brien started writing letters to them—something he'd be able to leave behind, like memories, fatherly advice, hopes. He feared that the boys might never really know who their aging father was or what he thought. He began writing letters about how proud he was of their skills in solving a Rubik's Cube, or about the good grades on their report cards, or how proud he was "of their acts of kindness and human decency." O'Brien says the letters were "to give Timmy and Tad what I have often wished my own father had given me—some scraps of paper signed 'Love, Dad.'"

O'Brien writes: "A younger father might tell his children he loves them sixty thousand times over a lifetime. I feel the pressure to cram those sixty thousand I-love-yous into a decade or so, just to reach my quota." His wife, Meredith, urged him to think about putting those letters together in the form of a book. "You don't have to commit to an actual book," she told him. "Just a maybe book. What you've written about fatherhood might mean something to other parents."

"Or to their kids," said Tad.

In 2019, seventy-three-year-old O'Brien published those letters in a memoir he titled *Dad's Maybe Book*. The final words in O'Brien's book were indeed: "I loved you. Dad."

How does this fit, you might ask? Just this: writing a letter to someone you love doesn't require both of you to be alive on this earth together at the same time. O'Brien wrote letters to his sons, intending them to read his words after he was gone. Those letters carried the same message of love they would have if he had read them aloud to Timmy and Tad as he was writing them.

If you write a letter to your person who died, the love, longing, and affection in your words are as real as if they were sitting with you. It may be a comfort to believe your person hears your words.

BAILEY

No single approach works for everyone when working with your feelings of loss. Bailey said she wanted to try to feel a connection to her sister Sydney. "Yes, I tried texting her," she said. "But I think it hurt more than helped because, obviously, there's no response. For me, it was just another reminder that she's not there anymore."

What to do with your letter, if you choose to write one? You can do anything you want with it:

- Keep it to yourself and save it on your computer.

- Print a copy and keep it with your journal.

- Send it to your person's email.

- Put the letter in an envelope, stick a stamp on it, and mail it to them, with your address on it.

- After you've written it, you can throw it away if you feel that helps to let go.

- Share it on your blog, a grief forum, or on a site like Grief Dialogues or AfterTalk.

WRITING DOWN YOUR DREAMS

Every night that we settle down to sleep, we each have between four and six dreams. During a solid eight hours, about two hours of that pillow time is spent with our minds spinning the stories and images of our dreams. There's mixed opinion on the meaning and purpose of dreams: some researchers say the mind is just sorting through the memories of our day, placing the details into memory file folders. Other researchers think that dreams are important processes where our subconscious is helping us work through problems and process our emotions. All that nighttime storytelling can be helpful when we're in the process of working through grief. Dreams can give us valuable insights about what we're going through, help us overcome fears, and even help deal with feelings of loss.

When someone close to us dies, it's common to have dreams about them. Dreams can be a space where we can have another connection with our person, perhaps one more encounter or a space to express love or regret. While some of those dreams can feel traumatic—maybe reliving the circumstances of their death—grief dreams are often beneficial. Those dreams can appear as a visit between you and your person. There may be a message that they have for you, which is often a message of reassurance—that they're okay and that you'll be okay, too. These dreams are a normal part of the grieving process, and they can bring a lot of comfort.

Most people have a hard time remembering their dreams, though. They may feel like they're "one of those people who just don't dream" (even though we all dream, whether we remember them or not). Or we may wake up and have the sense of having dreamt—but if we jump right out of bed to get ready for school or work, that dream can just drift away like smoke.

Writing down your dreams can help in a couple of ways: By getting into the practice of writing them down, you'll find that your ability to remember your dreams will improve. What might at first be a thin morning memory of a place or an object or a scene can, after just a little practice, become a fully developed story or encounter that you can recall in great detail.

When you improve your ability to remember your dreams and begin to write them down, you'll be able to make them more enduring, be able to see patterns, and have the benefit of a record of your dream encounters with your person. Here are some tips to help you remember your dreams enough to write them down:

- As you're lying down for the night, remind yourself that you want to remember your dreams.

- Keep a notebook and pencil on your nightstand.

- If you can, try not to use an alarm clock, which will jolt you awake. You want to wake up quietly and gently.

- When you wake up in the morning, don't immediately get out of bed. Lie quietly with your eyes closed, and see what images are floating around. You may think of yourself as sitting in a theater and looking at a blank movie screen—as if you're waiting for the film to start. Scan your mind and watch the screen for any snippet, thread, or image you can recall.

- No matter how small or seemingly irrelevant the detail, jot it down in your notebook.

- Keep your focus on that one detail or image. You'll find that there
will be another image connected to it, and then another. Think of
it like this: You're in a fog and holding on to a string (the detail
or image). As you pull on the string and reel it in, you'll find that
another image is connected to it, and then another. Finally, you'll
see a full-fledged scene and story rising out of the fog. Reel it in on
the end of your string, and write down the details.

Be patient and consistent. The first couple of times, you might not
remember any dream images, or maybe just one or two. But stick with
it. Before long, you'll be remembering and writing down three or four
dreams every morning. You'll be filling up your notebook with rich and
detailed dreams that reveal how your sleeping mind is trying to help you
work through the feelings you're having. Somewhere in those dreams
you're now able to remember and write down, you may even find your
person.

FINDING THE NARRATIVE OF OUR OWN LIVES

As we're talking about all these different kinds of writing—journals,
fiction, essays, and dreams—do they all tie together? When we think
about our lives as not just "the things that happen to us," but as "the
stories we tell ourselves about the things that happen to us," all of these
different kinds of writing can come together to help us work through
grief in an integrated way.

In her TED Talk "How Changing Your Story Can Change Your
Life," psychotherapist Lori Gottlieb took a break from writing her
advice column in the *Atlantic* magazine to share ideas about how we
often make sense of our lives by thinking of them as stories. That story
might be: "I'm a fifteen-year-old girl who plays on my school's soccer
team, and I have a ton of friends." Or "I'm a seventeen-year-old guy
who reads everything I can get my hands on and loves to be outside in
the woods."

We define ourselves and keep consistency in our lives by repeating these story lines to ourselves, and that's a good thing. What if, as Gottlieb says in her TED Talk, the stories we tell ourselves are incomplete or just aren't serving us well anymore? What if the stories we tell ourselves are keeping us stuck, instead of giving us clarity and helping us live fully?

Gottlieb says, "We assume that our circumstances shape our stories. But what I found time and again in my work is that the exact opposite happens. The way we narrate our lives shapes what they become." We typically feel like we have all kinds of freedom—until we have a big problem in front of us, and then we feel trapped by our circumstances. We feel like we're behind bars that we can't get through. Grief can feel that way—our person has died, and nothing can change that. It feels so final and so everlasting, and like this pain will never stop.

It's possible, though, to view our circumstances as part of our life—our narrative. When we're in a place where we cannot control our circumstances, we can change our story or how we view our circumstances. Your journaling, fiction writing, essays, letters to your person, and writing down your dreams can help you "test-drive" a different story. If your story has been "I'm a kid who has lost her father, and I'll never be happy again," is it possible to rewrite that story to something like "My father died too young, and I've been able to honor his memory and all he taught me by carrying his name forward"?

If the story you've run in your mind has been keeping you behind bars, Gottlieb suggests that you can "let go of the one version of the story you've been telling yourself so that you can live your life and not the story that you've been telling yourself about your life. And that's how we walk around those bars."

Allowing ourselves to write creatively gives us a way to explore our minds—our pain and joy, our fears and hopes, and can help us find our way to the new story of our lives. We can rewrite that story in a way that honors our person who's died and gives us a way to walk around the bars that have been keeping us stuck.

CREATING WITH ART

B. J. Miller is a doctor with the Zen Hospice Project in San Francisco, where he helps people who are nearing the end of their lives. Miller has had his own experiences with loss and grief and has some perspectives on how art has helped him find his way forward.

In 1990 when he was a nineteen-year-old college sophomore, Miller was goofing around with friends after a late night on the town. They climbed on top of a parked commuter train where an electrical current arced to the metal wristwatch Miller was wearing. The eleven thousand volts that surged through him caused him to lose his left arm and both legs below the knees.

Just as we experience grief in the loss of someone we love, Miller experienced a type of grief when he lost his limbs. With so much of his body now missing, he even wondered whether he was still fully human. In a podcast conversation with author Tim Ferriss (see the resources section), Miller talked about how he looked at his body and saw so much he wanted to change but couldn't. Even though he couldn't change what had happened to his body, he realized that there was something he could change. He could change his perspective. Art was something that helped him do that. Miller said:

> Art is inherently kind of useless, and that seems to be part of its charm. So that seemed to me—the fact that we as a species make art and care about it, seemed to me important because I was trying to figure out, "Well, who am I now? Am I less human because I have fewer body parts? Is that the measure of what it means to be a human being?" No, but I couldn't really answer the question . . . [of] why was I happy to be still alive. Those are the kinds of questions I was trying to kind of wade through. Essentially, questions of identity.

In her book *Big Magic: Creative Living beyond Fear*, author Elizabeth Gilbert echoes this observation that something like "art" is so important to us, even though it's essentially useless in helping us survive. Gilbert writes:

> Consider this fact: The earliest evidence of recognizable human art is forty thousand years old. The earliest evidence of human agriculture, by contrast, is only ten thousand years old. Which means that somewhere in our collective evolutionary story, we decided it was way more important to make attractive, superfluous items [art] than it was to learn how to regularly feed ourselves.

So, how can something like art, which some people might call "useless," help us work the process of grief? For Miller, whether looking at paintings or listening to music, he found that art was about learning to listen, learning how to see things in different ways, and having the choice to assign meaning to what he saw on the canvas.

Miller found that interpreting art was strengthening his ability to see new perspectives, which translated to his ability to look at his new reality with fresh eyes. He began to understand that he could survive the devastating injuries he'd suffered but still be able to go back into the world and find a sense of wholeness. He told Ferriss:

> [Art] helps you learn how to see, how to listen. That was really empowering because there's so much I would have loved to change about what I was seeing. When I looked at my body, I would have loved to have changed so much about it. But I couldn't. But with this knowledge, I could change my perspective. I could change how I saw myself. That's what art helped me learn and where to focus my energies. It's really paid off.

When we lose a person in our life, there's so much that we'd like to go back and change too. If we lose a mother, we've lost that part of us that was "a son" or "a daughter." We've lost not only that person we love, but we've lost an important part of ourselves—kind of like how Miller felt when losing his limbs.

In moving toward wholeness, the processes sound remarkably similar. If art could help Miller find meaning and new perspectives after such great loss, art can probably help us too. The process of creating art gives you a way to express thoughts and feelings in a way that transcends the spoken or written word. Whether you're experimenting with painting in oils or watercolors, sculpting in clay, carving in wood, or taking photographs, creating images can allow you to draw or paint or sculpt the emotions that may be too hard to write. In form, you can show the feelings for which you just can't find the words.

Sometimes, just the physical process of creating art can be helpful. There's an emotional release you can feel in slapping the paint onto the canvas, kneading the clay between your hands, or carving away slivers of wood.

If you feel a sense of darkness and helplessness, perhaps depicting those hard emotions in a piece of art can both help other people understand how you're feeling and help you shine some light on those dark places. In your art, you might illustrate a scene that represents a good memory of you and your person that will give you a way to memorialize and crystallize that bright memory of them.

By turning the emotions, thoughts, and feelings into art, you can work with your memories to honor your person who died and depict hopes, new meanings, and how a new relationship with your person might look. If you stick with the practice of creating over time, you also give yourself a record of your journey of transformation and finding meaning. Novelist Raymond Chandler wrote, "In everything that can be called art, there is a quality of redemption."

Many grief support groups provide resources to give youth a place to work with art as part of the healing process. Places like the Dougy Center in Portland, Oregon, provide an art room where kids and teens can create and explore their feelings through drawing and painting.

> ## GRACE
>
> Thirteen-year-old Grace found that the art room at Brooke's Place in Indianapolis, Indiana, gave her a place where she could draw and work with whatever she was feeling at the time. It gave her a sense of control that she could draw what she wanted, and that she could share her art, or not share. It was up to her. "They have a room with tons of art supplies where you can just sit and draw anything you'd like," Grace said. "If you want to show your drawing around and tell people about it, you can. But you can also keep it for yourself if it's a drawing just for you."

In her TED Talk "How Loss Helped One Artist Find Beauty in Imperfection," artist Alyssa Monks talks about how painting helped her work with the grief she felt in losing her mother. Alyssa says:

We're all going to have big losses in our lives, maybe a job or a career, relationships, love, our youth. We're going to lose our health, people we love. These kinds of losses are out of our control. They're unpredictable, and they bring us to our knees. And so I say, let them. Fall to your knees. Be humbled. Let go of trying to change it or even wanting it to be different. It just is. And then there's space, and in that space feel your vulnerability, what matters most to you, your deepest intention. And be curious to connect to what and who is really here, awake and alive. It's what we all want.

Alyssa's art and her painting gave her "the opportunity to find something beautiful in the unknown, in the unpredictable, and even in the awful."

When working with art—whether painting or scrapbooking or sculpting or photography—perhaps you can also find a way forward into the unknown and the unpredictable, and find some beauty there, too.

LISTENING TO MUSIC

Music has a powerful effect on our emotional experience. Is there anyone among us who hasn't felt an adrenaline surge at the dramatic opening of a favorite song? The drums and keyboards that begin Led Zeppelin's "Kashmir" can make you feel like you're flying over an exotic mountain range. Or you might feel a different kind of joyful elevation when queuing up "Happy" by Pharrell Williams.

We use music to help us relieve stress, provide an atmosphere, or change our mood. It may be background music at a party, cranking up the car stereo with the windows down, or soft music to help us concentrate while doing homework. Some studies show that listening to music activates our brain's dopamine system, which is responsible for the pleasurable responses we have to other pleasant experiences like sitting down to a favorite food or settling in to watch a crimson sunset.

Listening to a favorite song that you and your person enjoyed together can help bring those good memories of them front and center. Listening to an oldie like Glen Campbell's "Gentle on My Mind" from your mom's playlist may bring the image of her singing along with Campbell when you were a little kid. Maybe your sister's favorite was Lady Gaga, and listening to her sing "Shallow" can make you feel like your sister is a little bit closer to you now.

LOGAN

Logan said, "What's really helped me, I think, has been music. I listen to a lot of the stuff my dad raised me on, the stuff he listened to in high school: AC/DC, Def Leppard, all those older rock-and-roll bands, and heavy metal bands like Metallica and Rob Zombie." After his dad died, Logan inherited the '72 Chevy pickup truck that they restored together. When Logan wants to feel close to his dad, he sits in the cab of the truck and listens to the music. "Me, I've grown a liking to country music," Logan said. "But with every bone in his body, my dad hated country. I'll be sitting in our pickup and turn on some country, and the next thing I hear is my dad's voice saying, 'You're not playing that in my truck!' But I do feel like it helps me get through my grieving process, like I'm keeping him alive through our traditions and through the music we used to listen to together."

DEXTER

This shared love has helped Dexter feel connected to his dad too. "My dad loved music," he said. "He had all these classic vinyl LPs, and he loved to tell me what he knew about the songs and the artists. This one time, I was wondering where the song 'One' came from. I thought Three Dog Night wrote it, but Dad was like, 'Oh no! Harry Nilsson wrote that.' Then he literally went all Rain Man on me—telling me all about who Harry Nilsson was, showing me Nilsson documentaries, buying me a box set of Nilsson's records. I can still name all of Nilsson's songs right now. I just loved how fanatical my dad was with his music. I have a really nice record player that he got me, and I like to pick from the boxes of his vinyl records from the '70s, the '60s, the '50s, the '40s, and even the 1930s."

While music can help us frame up pleasant memories, music can also help us embrace the harder feelings and emotions that come with the loss of our person who died. Letting those feelings stay bottled up can keep us stuck, and music is one way to help get those emotions moving. Like Anne Lamott said in her TED Talk: "Tears will bathe and baptize and hydrate and moisturize you and the ground on which you walk." Tears can lubricate, too, and help remove the friction that may be keeping your emotions jammed up inside of you. Listening to music that expresses the depths of sadness and longing and loss can help us get in touch with those emotions and let them flow through. The more we can let those feelings find their way out of us and into the light, the less we need to carry them with us. Music and songs that allow you to get in touch with your grief and get it moving might include some like these:

- "If We Were Vampires" by Jason Isbell: "It's knowing that this can't go on forever; Likely one of us will have to spend some days alone."

- "Come Wake Me Up" by Rascal Flatts: "Tonight your memory burns like a fire" and "I just sit in these flames and pray that you'll come back, close my eyes tightly, hold on and hope that I'm dreaming."

- "Supermarket Flowers" by Ed Sheeran: "A heart that's broke is a heart that's been loved. So I'll sing Hallelujah, you were an angel in the shape of my mum. A life with love is a life that's been lived."

- "Colder Weather" by the Zac Brown Band: "I want to see you again, but I'm stuck in colder weather. I'm with your ghost again. It's a shame about the weather, but I know soon we'll be together."

- "Angel Flying Too Close to the Ground" by Willie Nelson: "So leave me if you need to / I will still remember / Angel flying too close to the ground."

- "Tears in Heaven" by Eric Clapton: "Would you know my name if I saw you in heaven? Would you be the same if I saw you in heaven?"

- "Timshel" by Mumford & Sons: "And death is at your doorstep, and it will steal your innocence. But it will not steal your substance. You are not alone in this."

- Adagio for Strings by Samuel Barber: In this piece of classical music without words, the soaring strings stop abruptly and then ease you gently back down to the ground. It can take you on a journey that will pull at your heart and let you connect with the poignant feelings of loss.

If part of the process of working through grief is being able to embrace the emotions of loss, using music can help. You might feel like priming the pump of tears might be too hard, might hurt too much. It may not be for everyone, but having a good cry can make you feel lighter, less burdened, and more open to reaching out.

DEXTER

Dexter said, "I'd tell another kid who's lost someone that it's not unusual to want to cry for no apparent reason—even if you're a guy. Maybe it sounds stupid, but I'm a guy, and I cry a lot—and I'm happy to admit it. For me, at those times, I feel a greater need for hugging and affection, maybe from my other mom or my really good friends."

Letting the music move you and having a good cry and letting it wring you out can give that grief someplace to go, and make room for something else where that grief used to live.

TUNING INTO PODCASTS

If you've been able to connect with a grief support group, you may have found a sense of community and belonging with a circle of other teens who know what it's like to experience the death of someone they love. It can be reassuring to tell your story, to share with others who've walked the same road and understand where you're coming from, and know that you're not alone in this.

Being able to listen to the stories of other kids' journeys can help a lot too. It can make you feel less alone when you hear someone share a story that makes you say, "I had that same experience" or "I've felt like that, too."

What if you haven't found the right group yet? Or maybe there aren't any grief support groups close to where you live? Or what if you're feeling more private about your grief right now, and don't want to feel the vulnerability of being in a group of other teens you don't know well (yet)? All those things don't mean that you have to miss out on conversations that could help you. You can find those kinds of conversations on podcasts. The resources section at the back of this book lists some suggestions, but here are a few podcasts to highlight:

- *Grief Out Loud*: This podcast is produced by the Dougy Center in Portland, Oregon. The center was named after Dougy Turno, a thirteen-year-old Oregon boy who had an inoperable brain tumor. Dougy inspired everyone around him with how he was able to bond with other kids and to help them talk about their fears about death and dying. The Dougy Center has kids and teens at the center of their mission, and their podcast is one way they reach out to connect and help kids work with their grief. Their podcasts are short, generally about thirty minutes long, and talk about topics like "Who Am I Now?" that my person has died. Or mini episodes where kids talk about their grief experiences. Or an episode on how humor and stand-up comedy helped one guy express his grief in a healthy way.

- *Open to Hope*: This podcast focuses on kids and families and is hosted by a mother-daughter team who are both therapists. The episodes are short and touch on topics like remembering siblings, dealing with the loss of a parent, or how Buddhist practices can help with healing.

- *What's Your Grief*: This podcast is part of the WhatsYourGrief.com website. The podcast's subtitle is *No Tilted Heads, No Soothing Tones, Just Real-World Grief Talk*. The hosts Eleanor and Litsa have bright and positive voices for easy listening. The episodes are practical and cover topics like going back to school after the death of someone you love, or the conflicting emotions that go along with grief, or how grief is handled in TV shows like *This Is Us* or *The Gilmore Girls*.

- "How Hearts Can Heal after Tragedy": Historian and religion professor Elaine Pagels talks with Terry Gross on her *Fresh Air* podcast. Gross talks with Pagels about her experience with grief after Pagels's six-year-old son died of a long illness, and then her husband died in a mountain-climbing accident a year later. She talks about how meditation and spiritual contemplation helped her to deal with grief in her life.

- On his podcast *The Tim Ferriss Show*, Tim speaks with B. J. Miller, the doctor at the Zen Hospice Project in San Francisco mentioned earlier in this chapter. In the episode titled "The Man Who Studied 1,000 Deaths to Learn How to Live," Miller talks about how working with dying people and their families and the experience of grieving the loss of his legs and one arm in an electrocution accident helped him find a way to live more fully, even in the face of great loss.

Many great conversations are waiting for you out there in podcasts. It's not the same as being in a room and talking with other teens who know grief. It's no substitute for finding a good counselor to talk to, but podcasts can give you insights into the experiences of others and how they've been able to work with grief and find a way forward with meaning and wholeness.

CONNECTING ON SOCIAL MEDIA

The internet can provide a great wealth of resources and connections. You can find videos and TED Talks about ways to approach grieving, reviews on books you feel could help you, and information on resources like support groups and online forums.

Social media can give us a way to stay connected with friends, share things we feel like we're ready to share, and follow along with people or organizations that provide uplifting messages, encouragement, or a sense of community. The flip side is that the web can be a source of distraction, and social media can often give a skewed perspective on how things are when people put only their best face forward.

Apps like Instagram, Twitter, Facebook, or Snapchat can give us a way to stay connected and to let our friends know how we're doing.

Sharing an update like "I'm really missing my brother today," "Feeling low . . . somebody tell me something good," or "I miss her as much today as yesterday, but today it hurts a little less" can open the door for your friends to offer some encouragement or understanding.

Sharing a line of poetry or a quote from a book you're reading, posting a photograph of that moment the sun breaks the horizon on your early-morning walk, or sharing a link to some music you're listening to—all those things give you a way to express what's inside of you. It's an invitation for your friends to respond and acknowledge that you're reaching out with something that means something to you.

DEXTER

Dexter has been able to look at both sides of the social media coin. He said, "On the positive side of being online, you can share how you're doing with people who can truly be sympathetic and are genuinely interested in how you're doing. And even if kids just want to relate to you in a friendly way, social media can be good for that." On the other hand, Dexter has seen how good judgment is important in deciding how much to share and being conscious of how he's presenting himself. "On the negative side," he said, "it's easy for there to be misunderstandings in what you post. People can look at what you're sharing and have these kinds of weird reactions, like 'Oh, they have someone dead in the family.' You have to use good judgment."

In general, our friends seem to have developed clear-eyed and mature understandings about what social media is good for, and the accompanying risks of posting online.

KATE

Kate recognized that we sometimes judge how we're doing by comparing ourselves to how other people are portraying their lives. "The problem with social media," Kate said, "is that people are posting things that put their best selves out there. They're not always showing what's going on inside." The writer Anne Lamott would probably agree with Kate when she wrote, "Never compare your insides to everyone else's outsides."

JDB

JDB is tracking right along with Kate and Anne Lamott. He said, "With social media, people are putting their best lives out there. You don't know what's really going on with people." JDB said that he doesn't spend a lot of time on social media. "I might go there to find news or to communicate with a couple of my friends. But I actually haven't posted anything in years—I really don't have anything I'd want to post."

GRACE

Even at the age of thirteen, Grace has the same insights as the older kids have been able to develop, and she uses social media sparingly. She said, "I think social media is a balance of both good and bad. I can use it to connect with my friends outside of school. When they post up things where I see them doing projects to help other kids, it's a positive thing that I can feel good about. But sometimes social media brings so much negative energy that it's unsettling, I'm pretty good about recognizing that point and seeing when it's time to get off. It's a mix of positive and negative."

Even with the negativity and the noise that can comprise social media, those apps can help with staying connected with friends and can provide a place to follow public figures or groups that can feed us with encouragement and insight and tools to help work through feelings of loss.

Some examples might include the Instagram page of David Kessler (@IamDavidKessler), the author of several books on the grief process (which you can find in the bibliography). Kessler posts regularly, with short videos, quotes, affirmations, and encouragement for self-care.

Same for the Grief Toolbox (@the_grief_toolbox), HealGrief (@heal grief), and several other pages that post regularly with affirmations and quotes that can lift you, or help you see that you're not alone. See the resources section for a listing of grief support pages to follow on social media.

ENTERING THE STORIES OF BOOKS AND MOVIES

Lots of self-help books are out there to help us understand grief and share ideas of how to work through it. Nonfiction books aren't the only ones that can help us understand the loss we feel, or to show us possible paths ahead. The fictional stories we find in novels and movies can sometimes be better guides through grief than "how-to" books; would you rather be told what to do or be shown a story that lets you see the options and potential paths for yourself?

Why do we go to the movies or enter the world of a novel? Do we go just to be entertained, amused, or distracted? That may be part of it. In Paul Auster's novel *The Brooklyn Follies*, a character says, "When a person is lucky enough to live inside a story, to live inside an imaginary world, the pains of this world disappear. For as long as the story goes on, reality no longer exists." Immersing ourselves into stories can be a kind of escape—we can leave our troubles behind for a little while and inhabit that other world.

Fictional stories give us something besides escape. Think about when you go to a movie theater and stand in front of the marquee. You look at the selection of films you can choose to watch: maybe an action-adventure or a romantic comedy. How about a horror film or a tragedy? We make our choice, we get our popcorn and our drink, and then we go in to find our seat. The lights go down, the movie starts, and the world outside disappears for ninety minutes. It all feels real, doesn't it? We flinch when the swords clang together. We laugh genuine laughter at the humor. We yelp with genuine fear when a villain crashes through the door. We cry real tears when the hero or heroine dies in battle. We're immersed in this other world that feels real while we're in it.

Then the lights come up, and the credits roll. We get up, leave the theater, and walk outside. We've been entertained for ninety minutes, but something else might have happened, too. We might have learned that we can feel real pain, genuine joy, true sorrow—even if they're hard or make us cry—and still be able to get up and keep moving forward. It's a small example that we can feel real emotions without being destroyed by them.

Maybe more important is that a story can give us ideas on how we might make our way through the world. In his memoir *My Reading Life*, novelist Pat Conroy (who also wrote *The Great Santini* and *The Prince of Tides*) says this about novels:

> From the beginning, I've searched out those writers unafraid to stir up the emotions, who entrust me with their darkest passions, their most indestructible yearnings, and their most soul-killing doubts. I trust the great novelists to teach me how to live, how to feel, how to love and hate. I trust them to show me the dangers I will encounter on the road as I stagger on my own troubled passage through the complicated life of books that try to teach me how to die.

If a novel can help a great writer like Conroy navigate a troubled passage on a hard road, novels might be able to help us too. Another great example comes from novelist Louise Erdrich in her book *The Painted Drum*, the story of an appraiser of Native American antiquities. The character is assessing an estate and decides to steal a painted Ojibwe drum and return it to the Ojibwe tribe. It's a novel where several characters are navigating their own experiences of grief. Erdrich writes:

> Life will break you. Nobody can protect you from that, and living alone won't either, for solitude will also break you with its yearning. You have to love. You have to feel. It is the reason you are here on earth. You are here to risk your heart. You are here to

be swallowed up. And when it happens that you are broken, or betrayed, or left, or hurt, or death brushes near, let yourself sit by an apple tree and listen to the apples falling all around you in heaps, wasting their sweetness. Tell yourself you tasted as many as you could.

Novels and movies can sometimes be better than self-help books in helping us figure out how to move through grief. Taste all of life that you can. In a story, nobody is telling you what you should do. The stories draw you into a world and introduce you to characters who are struggling with conflict and grief and meaning, just like you are—just like we all are. When you see Oskar in the movie *Extremely Loud & Incredibly Close*, searching all over New York for something that can help him connect with his father who died in 9/11, you might feel less alone knowing that you're not the only one who'd go to great lengths to stay connected.

KATE

Our friend Kate has found comfort in books and stories. "I liked *Siddhartha* by Hermann Hesse," she said. "It's a great book about reaching enlightenment and how you have to go through trials to reach it. And how there's not just one way, but different paths to get there. I also liked *The Epic of Gilgamesh*. I love immersing myself into a world that is so different from mine, but also has so many similarities—you can see that even people from long ago were struggling—and how in the end, they're able to persevere."

DEXTER

Not every story has to have some deep purpose or tell a tale of somebody finding their way through great adversity. Sometimes it's good enough for stories to take us out of what we're dealing with, to entertain us, and give us a break. Dexter said he doesn't care much for weighty or depressing stories. "When I pick up a book," he said, "I prefer action or adventure. Or even a mystery . . . mysteries are always fun."

Apart from providing some kind of template on how to navigate grief, or giving us relief by letting us enter another world of action or mystery, sometimes the value of a story is that it provides us with a chance to get emotions unstuck. A movie that connects with us emotionally can help us feel like we're not the only one to have had this sadness. A good cry can be a good thing.

JDB

JDB talked about a movie that meant a lot to him after his father died. "The movie was called *Hachi: A Dog's Tale*. The dad finds this abandoned dog in the subway system and brings the dog home," JDB said. "The two of them really bond. The dad would go to work, and the dog would wait at the train station for the dad to come home. The dad died at work one day, maybe a heart attack or something, we don't really know. For years, the dog just kept coming to the station, waiting for him. It was a movie that really hit me."

Stories can show us we're not alone or give us an escape from having to think about our sadness, or they can tell us a relatable story that helps us get our feelings flowing. Sometimes popular television shows can offer nuggets of wisdom and insight that can give us different ways to think about grief. The NBC family drama *This Is Us* is a popular show that has many themes of grief woven through its connecting story lines. The series revolves around the lives of Rebecca and Jack Pearson, who start their family when Rebecca is having triplets. During the birth of the triplets, Kevin and Kate survive, but the third child Kyle does not. Jack and Rebecca are devastated to lose their infant son. Before they leave the hospital with Kevin and Kate, Jack and Rebecca discover that there's another child in the nursery, born the same day but abandoned outside a fire station. They decide to adopt this baby and name him Randall.

In a great scene (the Season 4 finale, "Strangers: Part Two"), Jack and Rebecca are throwing a first birthday party for one-year-old Kate, Kevin, and Randall. They find themselves unexpectedly overcome with grief for Kyle, whom they never got a chance to know. Jack and Rebecca, confused by their conflicted feelings of happiness and sadness, decide to drop in unannounced on their family physician, Dr. Katowski, who had delivered Kevin, Kate, and Kyle. They're hoping the kindly old doctor will be able to help them with some wisdom or perspective.

Dr. K sits them in his office, the one-year-olds in their strollers, and tells them his own story about losing his first child. He used to sing to his wife's belly, he tells them. "Blue skies, smilin' at me, nothin' but blue skies do I see. . . ." When Dr. K and his wife lost that child, they listened to that song over and over, and it made them sad as if they were listening to "Blue Skies" just to punish themselves.

When his wife got pregnant again, Dr. K says, he found himself surprised to be singing again to his wife's belly—and singing that very same song to this unborn child. "And then twenty-five years later, I danced with my daughter to that song at her wedding." He goes on:

> That song, ahh. . . . It made us happy; it made us sad; it made us happy again. The whole human experience just wrapped up in that one song. Hospitals are kind of like that, you know—these bizarre buildings where people experience some of their greatest joys and some of their most awful tragedies, all under one roof. I think the trick is not trying to keep the joys and the tragedies apart. But you kinda got to let 'em cozy up to one another. You know, let 'em coexist. And I think that if you can do that, if you can manage to forge ahead with all that joy and heartache mixed up together inside of you, never knowing which one is gonna get the upper hand, well, life does have a way of shaking out to be more beautiful than tragic.

Finding insights like "the trick is letting the joys and sorrows cozy up and coexist" might almost make television worth watching again.

EMBRACING POETRY

Rita Dove says that "poetry is language at its most distilled and most powerful." As a U.S. poet laureate and Pulitzer Prize–winning poet, she'd be a good one to know: the imagery and metaphors in a good poem can connect with us on a personal and universal level.

Lots of people think that poetry isn't for them, and that can be understandable. Poetry can be hard, but if you give some poems or poets a chance, you might find that they're revealing some deep truths, often in very few words. While it might take an hour to read a short story or a week to read a novel, a poem can be a concentrated experience of emotion, insight, and meaning that you can digest in five or ten minutes. If you're looking for solace and perspective in working through grief, poems might be a good place to look.

Robert Frost was also awarded a Pulitzer Prize for Poetry—the only poet to receive that recognition four times. When asked about the meaning and value of poetry, he said, "A poem begins with a lump in the throat, a homesickness, or a love-sickness. It is a reaching-out toward expression, an effort to find fulfillment. Poetry is when an emotion has found its thought, and the thought has found words." That sounds like a straight line from the heart to the page and back again—from the poem to your heart.

As a way to help us work through the grief of losing someone we love, reading a poem that connects with emotion can help by showing you that you're not alone with what you're feeling. If the poet could write it, you know that plenty of other people have probably had those same feelings too. Dylan Thomas wrote that poetry can show us that "your bliss and suffering is forever shared." If you can feel like your suffering is shared, you don't have to carry it all alone.

Sometimes people feel intimidated by poetry, thinking that poems might be too complicated or hard to understand. Some poems might be obscure, but Henry David Thoreau said that "good poetry seems too simple and natural a thing that when we meet it, we wonder that all men are not always poets. Poetry is nothing but healthy speech."

A few examples can show how poetry offers helpful insights in simple and natural language. This poem, "A Parable of Immortality" (also sometimes called "Gone from My Sight"), attributed to Reverend Luther F. Beecher, is often shared in hospice settings:

> I am standing upon the seashore.
> A ship at my side spreads her white sails to the morning breeze,
> and starts for the blue ocean.
> She is an object of beauty and strength,
> and I stand and watch her until she hangs like a speck of white cloud
> just where the sea and sky come down to mingle with each other.
> Then someone at my side says: "There! She's gone!"
> Gone where? Gone from my sight—that is all.
> She is just as large in mast and hull and spar
> as she was when she left my side,
> and just as able to bear her load of living freight
> to the place of her destination.
> Her diminished size is in me, and not in her.
> And just at the moment
> when someone at my side says: "There! She's gone!"
> there are other eyes that are watching for her coming;
> and other voices ready to take up the glad shout:
> "Here she comes!"
> And that is dying.

It's simple, clearly spoken, and gives us a little shift in perspective on how to look at the death of someone close to us.

Or maybe turn to Emily Dickinson's poem "Hope Is the Thing with Feathers" for a glimpse into how hope can carry us through to the other side of a storm. She writes: "'Hope' is the thing with feathers / That perches in the soul / And sings the tune without the words / And never stops—at all." Her message seems clear: Keep singing. Your soul needs the song of your hope. You'll make it through.

Some of our friends have found that writing poetry helps them work with the things they're feeling.

KATE

Kate said that while she's cautious about committing raw and honest words to a journal or essay, she finds that poetry is a bit different for her. What comes out in her poetry has a different flavor than her journaling. "When I write in the form of poetry, sometimes I'll feel like I want to save that for later," Kate said.

GRACE

Song lyrics are a form of poetry. Grace enjoys stage performing and likes to sing. "I've been trying to write music about how I feel," she said. "I don't think I'm good at it, but I like trying. If you stare at it hard enough, the words will change, and they'll start to sound good, though."

If you feel like writing poetry, you can keep it simple. If you want to learn about iambic pentameter or how many syllables should be in each line of a haiku, knock yourself out. But if you want to write free verse poetry, you're not bound by any constraints or patterns or cadences or anything like that. Your poems don't even have to rhyme.

Raymond Carver is thought to be one of the best American short-story writers and poets ever. In his 1989 poem "What the Doctor Said," a man is listening as his doctor is giving him the bad news about his diagnosis:

> he said I counted thirty-two of them on one lung before
> I quit counting them
> I said I'm glad, I wouldn't want to know
> about any more being there than that.

No rhymes. Nothing flowery. Just simple words about a person dealing with shock and fear. Carver then follows with the doctor asking the man a question:

> he said are you a religious man do you kneel down
> in forest groves and let yourself ask for help
> when you come to a waterfall
> mist blowing against your face and arms
> do you stop and ask for understanding at those moments
> I said not yet, but I intend to start today

If you were to write a poem about what you feel about your mother dying of cancer or your best friend taking her own life, what might that poem look like?

If we wanted to quote one more Pulitzer-winning laureate on the value of poetry—whether we're reading it or writing it—we could turn to Robert Penn Warren, who wrote in 1958:

> The poem is a little myth of man's capacity of making life meaningful. And in the end, the poem is not a thing we see—it is, rather, a light by which we may see—and what we see is life.

PRACTICING GRATITUDE

When we're suffering the pain of loss, it can feel like there's no reason to feel grateful. It may even feel like if we let ourselves feel gratitude for anything, it would feel like a betrayal of our person.

Gratitude is a powerful thing, and there's a lot of healing that can be found in the practice of cultivating it—of recognizing the things around us that are worthy of gratitude. On his YouTube channel, author and meditation expert Sam Harris offers up the short video "A Lesson on Gratitude" (which also appears in his Waking Up meditation app). Harris describes an exercise he sometimes practices when he finds himself disturbed by something wrong in his life:

> I sometimes think of bad things that haven't happened to me. I might think that I haven't been diagnosed with a fatal illness. I'm not caught in a war zone. And I think of all the people on earth in that moment who are suffering, those sorts of dislocations in their lives. And then I reflect that if I were in their shoes, I would be desperate to get back to precisely the situation I'm now in.

Cultivating a sense of gratitude is not about comparing loss, or trying to offer yourself a consolation prize, but instead allowing your attention to rest on the things around you that are worth appreciating. Those things are always there if you slow down to look.

JDB

JDB found that it's helped him to let his mind rest on the gratitude he feels for the time that he was able to share with his dad. "They say to try to think of the happy memories. Well, I did, and it helped," he said. "But it also hurts sometimes to think about those happy memories. I could feel like 'Man, I'm so glad I had such a great time with him.' But any of those good memories are also mixed in with knowing that those are times I won't be able to have with him again. And sometimes that hurts a lot more."

LOGAN

Logan practices gratitude by reaching out to appreciate the people he meets in the course of his day, the way he remembers his dad doing. Logan said, "Last week, I went to put in my paycheck in the bank. The bank teller asked me if I needed anything else. I just said, 'Yeah, I'll take a smile.' It was something my dad used to do all the time. It made the rest of my day great. It was a way to remember him. It made the bank teller smile, and I was smiling all the way out the door, too."

In his 1985 novel *Love in the Time of Cholera*, the writer Gabriel García Márquez reflects that the character of Dr. Juvenal Urbino had not yet learned that "the heart's memory eliminates the bad and magnifies the good, and that thanks to this artifice, we manage to endure the burden of the past." Many of our friends said they were able to find a sense of gratitude by holding on to good memories of the times they had with their person when they were alive.

DEXTER

Dexter talked about when he was twelve years old and went on a seven-month trip around the world with his family. The first half was with both his parents, but the second half was just Dexter and his dad. "We started in Asia, and then went to Bali and Taiwan. We went to some of the islands around Malaysia, then over toward Rome, Spain, and France. Then Turkey, the UK, Ukraine, and even down to Australia. I'm really glad I carry those memories of him."

LOGAN

Logan said that things hadn't always been great between him and his dad. "He'd been in a really bad motorcycle accident, and there were painkillers, so that caused a lot of conflict," Logan said. "But I've been able to let go of a lot of that. I like to put my thoughts on the car shows we'd go to when I was growing up, and the project cars and motorcycles we'd work on together. He was a motorcycle guy, and he looked the part," Logan said. "His name was Marcus, but some of his friends called him 'Mohawkus.' My favorite time of year is spring and summer when the Harleys come out, when the classic cars come out, when the car shows start. All those things that bring back good memories of doing stuff, me and my dad."

JDB

Being in the outdoors brings up memories of times that JDB feels thankful for. "Even though my dad was older, he was really active.

I liked to hear his stories of the crazy stupid stuff he would do as a kid, like him jumping off a bridge into a river, or him and his buddies throwing firecrackers at each other on the Fourth of July. Just dumb stuff like that. He'd take me down to his college roommate's lake house during the summer. I'm just grateful for the memories doing fun stuff like waterskiing or wakeboarding or tubing with him." JDB paused when talking about the good summer memories with his dad and reflected how it's not always an easy matter to stick with one emotion over another or to maintain optimism. "There's that joke that even if a kid's parents are going through a divorce, you can be optimistic and say, 'Well, now you get to have two Christmases,'" he said. "But when my dad died, it was hard to be optimistic about anything. After a couple of years, though, I felt like I could appreciate the brighter side of knowing that I'd met so many nice people during all I'd gone through. I'm really tight with the people in my support group at Brooke's Place." JDB would probably like Ralph Waldo Emerson's quote: "Cultivate the habit of being grateful for every good thing that comes to you and to give thanks continuously. And because all things have contributed to your advancement, you should include all things in your gratitude."

So many other great writers and philosophers have had insightful and practical things to say about how we can help ourselves bear the pain of living by embracing gratitude for all the things that happen to us. Because as Emerson said, all the things that happen to us have helped to make us who we are today, and who we're becoming.

The Stoic philosophers from Greece and Rome offered practical ways to think about pain and loss and misfortune and all the other "bad" things that happen to us in these lives. Epictetus was a slave and endured a lot of misfortune. He said, "Do not seek for things to happen the way you want them to; rather, wish that what happens happens the way it happens: then you will be happy."

Marcus Aurelius was a Stoic, as well as a Roman emperor and general. In his journals to himself, he wrote, "A blazing fire makes flame and brightness out of everything that is thrown into it." In more modern days, the German philosopher Friedrich Nietzsche wrote about what he called *amor fati*—a "love of fate." He wrote, "That one wants nothing to be different, not forward, not backward, not in all eternity. Not merely bear what is necessary, still less conceal it . . . but love it."

Nietzsche and Emerson and the Stoics are all pointing to the same idea. We have the capacity within ourselves to embrace all the experiences that life gives us. We can recognize that even the bad things that happen to us are part of what we throw onto the fire to build up the flame of life inside of us. If we choose to do so, we can look at all these experiences and have an element of gratitude that they're part of this ride we're on, and what's making us who we are becoming? It's not so easy an idea to embrace—having gratitude for even the painful things we experience. Deep thinkers have been writing about it for more than two thousand years, so there might be something to it.

We could go back to Sam Harris for another modern example. In his talk on gratitude, Harris is recounting a recent evening at the dinner table with his wife and two kids. They'd each of them had a bad day and were feeling pretty grumpy about it. Harris noticed how little joy they were all taking in being together:

> Then I thought . . . if I had died yesterday and could have the opportunity to be back with my family, I thought of how much I would savor this moment right now. And it totally transformed my mood. It gave me instantaneous access to my best self, and a feeling of pure gratitude for the people in my life. Just think of what it would be like to lose everything and then be restored to the moment you're now in, however ordinary. You can reboot your mind in this way, and it need not take any time. The truth is, you know exactly what it's like to feel overwhelming gratitude for your life.

Would your person want you to suffer or be unhappy? Or would they want you to live fully, with a sense of gratitude and meaning and purpose? Would they want that part of themselves to endure through you and in your memory, as a person with an appreciation for the life you're living now?

CHAPTER ELEVEN

REACHING OUT FOR HELP

R eaching out for help might feel like the last thing on your mind when you're swimming in the loss of your person dying. You can find tons of reasons to avoid asking for help. You might want to appear strong, showing everyone you've got a handle on everything. Sometimes it might feel easier to keep your feelings bottled up, to try to hide from the pain. Do any of these things sound familiar when you think about opening up to other people?

- "I don't want to lose my grip and cry in front of people."

- "I should be able to handle this on my own."

- "I don't want to deal with people."

- "Nobody could even understand what I'm going through."

- "It's easier not to rub salt in my wounds by talking about my person who died."

- "If I put a lid on it and stuff my feelings, maybe they'll just get better on their own."

- "I don't know where I'd even reach out."

- "I don't want to get asked a bunch of questions or feel obligated to offer some kind of comfort to other kids talking about their loss."

All people—even adults—have these thoughts when considering whether to reach out for help and talk about their grief. There's a risk, though, to staying folded up within ourselves and not reaching out. U.S. senator John McCain and South African political leader Nelson

Mandela both said that of all the things they suffered while impris-
oned, the worst thing they experienced was solitary confinement. Does
it make sense to put ourselves in solitary when we're trying to work
through the grief of losing someone we love?

We started out talking about how "you are not alone," right? Very
few people—if any—travel the road of grief alone. There are plenty of
good reasons to reach out and risk vulnerability in letting others help
you. We need other people. We need each other if we hope to move
forward and toward healing.

There are so many ways to reach out and find support. It's not a
one-size-fits-all kind of deal. Our friends had a lot to say about what has
worked for them and what hasn't. Some of them had to try a couple of
different approaches before they found the right kind of help for them.
Some of them found that support groups were just what they needed.
Some of them had better luck in developing a relationship with a counselor and having one-on-one conversations.

The first step to reaching out for support may not be as hard or
scary as you think. You can start by talking to the adults in your life
whom you trust and who care about you:

- A parent or adult in your home

- A minister or youth group leader

- Teacher or school counselor

- Older sibling

- Sports coach

- Aunt or uncle

- Primary care doctor

An open and honest conversation with an adult you trust can help
shed some light on the next best steps for you. Check the resources section at the back of this book for some ideas of where to look for help.

For example, websites of organizations like the Dougy Center in Portland, Oregon, or the National Alliance for Grieving Children provide "Grief Resources" that let you search by city or state and list hundreds of grief support centers and programs around the country. This is one good way to find a support group near you.

If groups aren't your thing, you may feel more comfortable talking with a grief therapist one-on-one. Talk to an adult you trust to help connect you with a professional who can work with you.

There's no single way that's right for everyone in working with the pain of grief. While we need others to help us on the path, different approaches work better for different kids. Here are some things that have worked for our friends.

FINDING A GRIEF SUPPORT GROUP

***

DEXTER

Sitting down and meeting with a bunch of other teens you don't know can be an intimidating thing. When Dexter and his mom found a grief support group at the Dougy Center, he wasn't too sure he wanted to get involved. "My mom told me it was a place for kids to talk about their grief," he said. "The first time I went, I did not want to go! I'll be honest, I was freaked out, and I was like, 'Who are these people? They won't understand me or get how hard the death of my dad is to me.'" Dexter's feelings aren't unusual. Who are these people, right? You think, "It's hard enough going to a party where I don't know the other people. Now I'm supposed to go into a room with a bunch of other kids who've also had someone die? There's probably going to be a lot of crying, and I'm not sure if I can handle any more of that."

***

Fair enough. Grief support groups involve kids coming together to talk about how they're doing, what's hurting and what's going well, what's helping them, and what's getting in the way. There might be some crying. You might feel vulnerable. They might feel vulnerable.

DEXTER

What Dexter found after just a couple of sessions was that sitting down and being able to share his feelings with other kids like him was a great help. He said, "I'm just glad to know that places like the Dougy Center are there for people. I just want to shout out its name to anybody who's had a tremendous loss or death of somebody close to them. Having a group has been a great help to me. These kids, these people, they understand. They have the same kind of weird vibe, and we just 'get' each other and understand what we're all going through."

Why do support groups work, and how do they work? Support groups might be six, eight, or a dozen kids around your age. They might meet once or twice a month and are usually led by a trained grief counselor. Groups like this can offer you a place to talk about your feelings and listen to other kids talk about how they're moving through their grief. These kinds of groups can give you a community of kids who can relate to what you're going through—because they've lost someone they love too.

GRACE

Talking to your other friends about how you're feeling is important, but sometimes it's hard for them to understand what you're going through. Grace said, "Most of the time, people who haven't lost a parent have a hard time relating to you, and they don't know how to respond. I started going to groups at Brooke's Place when I was four, a few months after my dad died. It's much, much different there. Having a support group like Brooke's Place has helped me open up so much, but I've seen it help so many other kids, too. I like seeing how new kids are able to open up over time as they join the group."

What are some things grief support groups can give you that may be hard to find with your other friends? Support groups can offer:

- Support and understanding from other kids who know what you're going through because they've experienced a similar loss

- A place where you can talk about how you're feeling without being judged

- The opportunity to start the healing process by sharing your story and being able to learn something from the stories of others

- Insights into coping skills that have worked for other kids your age, things that have helped them get through the tough days

- Ideas about how to keep your person present with you and make them a part of your life as you continue to live and find meaning

- Some perspectives on how other kids have navigated relationships with their other family members or with their friends

- As you grow and learn about yourself through this process of telling stories, you might find that you're becoming the experienced mentor, and can be able to help other kids by sharing what you've learned.

- Other teens in a support group are more likely to understand what you're going through. They won't judge you. They've been where you are. In those groups, you're not alone.

Many of our friends have found community, understanding, friendship, and healing in the grief support groups they've attended.

JDB

JDB described his experience with his support group at Brooke's Place in Indianapolis, Indiana. He said, "We meet every two weeks.

You always start by saying your name, and then saying the name of who you're there for—so you never forget them. We go around the table saying what were our highs of the last two weeks: what's been going good, stuff like that. Then we can talk about what's been our "lows"—what's not been going good or what we can improve. It's nice to see how other people are going through it. If they need help, you might be able to say something that helped you in a similar situation."

DEXTER

In support groups, there's no obligation to talk if you don't feel like it. When Dexter started going to his meetings after his dad died, his mom would drive him two hours each way to get there. He said, "It had been a little while since my dad died, but I was still feeling frantic. The people at the Dougy Center were inviting and so comforting to talk to. I was finding other kids who knew what I was going through, because they'd been through their own loss, too. In the groups, kids might not want to speak some nights, which was okay. They showed up, and they were supporting the other kids. Sometimes I might not feel like speaking, but when I do, I always feel better. And I'll think how maybe one of the other kids in my group might be feeling this way, too, and how it might help them to hear me. . . . We take people into the group like they're brothers and sisters, like it doesn't matter where you're from," Dexter said. "We understand you've had a significant loss, and nobody's going to judge you or judge how your person died."

JDB

JDB has a similar experience of how his support group allowed him to share and be understood but also to be able to learn from the experiences of other kids. He said, "I started in the ten-to-twelve age group, but we eventually merged into the teen group, and that's when it got way better. I got to sit in with the kids who were sixteen or seventeen or eighteen. It helps when you're only thirteen, and you can hear from the older kids who've been working through their grief for maybe five or six years already. It helped to hear those other kids' stories. There was one kid whose father passed away due to alcohol, and then his mom passed away from something else. He'd been living with his aunt, but he was one of the happiest kids there. He was always optimistic and making jokes. It's just kind of amazing to me to see it. It helps to surround yourself with people like that, and being able to see that people can lose people they love, and still live with it."

GRACE

Even though the groups can be meaningful and lead toward healing, the sessions aren't always easy. Grace said, "The groups can be hard. One time, we were all crying, but we all felt like a family. We were all relating to each other, and we all understood each other's pain. We felt sad but in a good way. We just felt safe in that room and knew that we could say whatever we felt was on our minds and in our hearts. Talking it out is good, and Brooke's Place has been a huge help for that."

JDB

Our friends have experienced a lot of healing and growth by talking with other kids in their support groups, especially when it's hard. JDB said, "There can be a lot of mood swings in the group, especially with the younger kids. But the more you keep going on, you can see their highs are getting better, and their lows are getting less frequent, which is really nice. I learn from other kids' stories and try not to make some of the mistakes they did. Being in a support group has helped me see that you can't just rush through your grief—it helps to see that you just have to go through it slowly, take your time, and do it naturally. When it's my turn to talk, sometimes I feel like I want to stay in my lane and not be a burden. But if I'm invited, and I can tell the other person is sincere in wanting to hear how I feel, it's easier for me to talk."

If you feel like a grief support group is something you think might be for you, check the resources section in the back of this book. Websites like the Dougy Center and the National Alliance for Grieving Children have their own resource sections, with searchable directories where you can find grief support groups near where you live. Check it out and talk it over with a trusted adult in your life.

GETTING A GOOD COUNSELOR

While joining a support group with other kids can help, sometimes sitting down with a trained and caring counselor is a good route too. It doesn't have to be an either/or option, though—nothing says you can't see a counselor and join a support group at the same time. Both can help you work with your feelings.

JDB

JDB does both and finds that while they serve different ends, they work together to help him find his way through his grief. "My group counseling has been good for talking with other kids and working with my grief about losing my father," he said. "The one-on-one counseling has been good for repairing other things, especially my relationship with my mom, which has gotten way better. We still have our arguments, but it's nothing major like it used to be. When I'm talking to my friends, there's always going to be some things I'm going to leave out. But with a one-on-one counselor, you can really be honest with them. They're there to listen and not judge you."

Many kinds of counselors can help. These might include social workers, school nurses or school counselors, pastors or ministers in your church, psychiatrists or psychologists, or counselors who specialize in working with kids experiencing the grief of losing someone they love.

BAILEY

Some teens feel more comfortable working with a single, trusted therapist. Bailey had tried a support group but found it wasn't for her. "I went to a grief group at school twice," she said. "I wasn't comfortable being public about my feelings, especially with people I don't know—even if they've gone through something similar to me. I felt like I ended up comparing my loss to everyone else's losses in the group, and I always felt like my loss was worse than theirs. I guess this made me feel out of place because it still felt like no one had been through what I was going through." Bailey found that by trusting her guidance counselor at school, she could open up a little easier and find some relief when she needed it. "I couldn't control when a trigger might show up and remind me of my sister, especially at school," Bailey said. "I ended up getting help from my guidance counselor, who was always there for me."

It can be reassuring to know that you have lots of options. There's no "right way to grieve" the death of someone you love, and no single path to finding your way through to the light. Just among our small group of friends in this book, it's clear they're each feeling free to choose the kind of help that's best for them.

So, personal preference is one reason to choose a counselor over group therapy or to add a counselor to the list of people who are helping you make your way forward. That's great; listen to yourself and choose the help that's best for you. Beyond personal preference and what your heart is telling you, are there other reasons you might consider seeking out counseling? Sure enough. Here are some things to keep on your radar. If you feel like some of these things apply to how you're feeling, a conversation with a trusted adult might be to help find a counselor who's right for you:

- The things you're trying in working with your grief don't seem to be helping.

- You might be thinking of hurting yourself or other people.

- Things seem hopeless, no matter what you're trying.

- Alcohol or drugs are becoming something you're using to try to lessen your pain.

- You're withdrawing from your friends or from social activities you've always enjoyed.

- Your sleep is messed up (you're sleeping all the time, or you can't sleep at all).

- You have a feeling of helplessness or purposelessness that won't go away.

- Other tough life events start to pile up on top of your grief: maybe you're breaking up with the person you're dating, or there's a family conflict or something else that makes it just too much to handle on your own.

Sometimes it can be tougher to ask for help from a counselor than it is to join a grief support group. Does going to see a counselor mean that you're weak or broken? Nothing could be further from the truth. Seeking out counseling when you need it is an act of courage. You're telling yourself that your life, and the memories and love you carry for your person who died, are things are worth fighting for. Your life and their memories are worth saving.

It's again helpful to listen to the different perspectives of our friends and to be reminded from their stories that there's no single path that's right for everybody. Kate found that a counselor worked better for her than talking with a group of other kids. JDB and Logan each found that a combination of their grief groups and individual counseling has helped each of them. Dexter is firmly in the group therapy camp, feeling that talking with other kids who understand him has been more helpful than sitting with a counselor.

KATE

Kate has spent her share of time talking with counselors, both one-on-one and in family counseling with her brother and two sisters. "A one-on-one counselor worked better in my case," she said. "Groups weren't my thing. I don't feel like I can focus if there's a bunch of people around me." Kate met with a couple of different counselors before she found the right match for her. She said, "What deters people from therapy is they don't find the right therapist. You have to be willing to try one and talk to them. If it doesn't work out, then go talk to another one until you find someone you feel safe and secure with. When I found my counselor Laura, it was an instant connection. I liked that she wasn't afraid to push me and tell me when I'm wrong . . . you don't want someone who's just going to agree with you all the time. She taught me some mindfulness exercises and how to home in on certain parts of myself. If you know that what you say is safe with your counselor, it can open you up to all levels of yourself. They can challenge you and act as an impartial third party in your mind. They can help you find tools to increase your own self-awareness. I think that's really important."

Kate makes a good point about the role of a counselor in working through issues of grief, or of any difficult life issues, for that matter. At their best, a counselor is not giving you answers, but rather helping you find the healing and wisdom that is already inside of you.

JDB

JDB understands this. He said, "Sometimes I'll be sitting there talking with my counselor, and not getting any answers. I came to see that that's kind of the point—you're not supposed to get answers fed to you. You're supposed to figure some of this stuff out on your own, find the answers inside you. I think that's one of the big things you have to realize."

LOGAN

Counseling can be a good option when other life events stack up and complicate your grieving process. Logan said his parents had a tough relationship when he was younger, and he spent a lot of time going to therapy even before his dad died. "My parents almost got divorced three times, so I just grew up going to therapy. Therapists were nothing new to me." When Logan started looking for help to bolster his group sessions at the Dougy Center, he looked for the right counselor to help him. "I found a specific therapist when I was a freshman," Logan said, "and I've been seeing her every week for the last four years. We work good together. My dad always taught me to bottle up my emotions, like he did. It made our relationship hard for the last three years of his life. But it doesn't work in the long run, because you need to take care of your emotions. When I started seeing my therapist, I was able to open up with her, and she helped me grow from there. Working with her has helped me to be more open with my mom. It's helped me be a lot more social and helps me deal with things."

A professional like a therapist can help you connect with other medical help if you need it. If you feel overly anxious or feel like your sadness is so deep that you feel like you need more help, a medical professional like a physician or nurse practitioner may be able to prescribe medication to help you get through a tough patch.

KATE

Kate said, "It's helped me to take an antidepressant or an antianxiety medication. Those kinds of medicines helped me deal with the pain I was feeling. If you're working in talk therapy and taking medicine together, and if it's prescri bed and you don't abuse it, it can be a happy medium, which I feel helped me."

DEXTER

Dexter recounted his views about counseling versus group therapy. "I did seek some one-on-one counseling, both through my school and a counselor outside of school," he said. "It helped for a little while, but they hadn't been through some of the trauma I'd been through. But I didn't feel like they helped me as much as going to group meetings with other kids at the Dougy Center. I got more out of talking with other kids who'd been through something traumatic themselves."

GRACE

Grace would agree that having a counselor who has personal experience dealing with loss and grief helped her connect. Even at the age of thirteen, she has the wisdom and insight of a kid who's spent most of her life working with the death of her dad when she was only four. Grace said, "It helps when you know that your counselor has had their own losses in life. It makes it so you're not only talking to an adult, but you're also talking with someone who's gone through the same kind of things as you."

If you feel like a counselor would be helpful in talking about your feelings about the death of your person, how would you go about finding a good fit for you? As always, you can reach out to a trusted adult in your life, and ask for help finding a good grief therapist. Sometimes, grief support groups also offer one-on-one counseling services. You could talk to friends who've lost someone in their lives and ask if they have a counselor they've liked. Talk to your family doctor or a school counselor for suggestions or referrals, or get on the web and do a search for "grief counseling" near where you live. Take what you've found to your trusted adult and let them help you find a counselor with whom you can relate.

It's a special relationship between you and a counselor: you'll be spending time together, talking about the hardest thing you've ever been through. So don't feel like you have to go with the first therapist you find. Listen to your gut and ask yourself if this person seems open to understanding your feelings. Have they had their own experience of someone close to them dying? Do you feel like you can be yourself, and that this therapist will listen without judging?

KATE

Will this therapist help you challenge yourself to get unstuck? Kate said about her therapist: "She wasn't afraid to push me and tell me if she thought I was wrong about something." A therapist can help challenge you to grow and look inside yourself, to places you might not rather look but which can help you heal. Give the therapist a chance, and see if you feel a level of trust. If they don't seem to be helping, you can always look for someone else.

Our friends give good examples that there's no single best way to reach out for help. You have choices to try what works best for you: one-on-one counseling or in a grief support group. Knowing that you have choices means that you have some control, and that might give you a feeling of empowerment and strength within you. Whichever way you choose, more healing is found in reaching out than hiding from your feelings. Nobody has to do this alone.

REACHING OUT TO HELP OTHERS

You've heard the refrain "You are not alone." You're not all by yourself in having to deal with the grief of losing someone you love. Other kids have had similar experiences before you and can help you with their gifts of empathy and example and insight. Grief counselors or therapists have trained for this. They've worked to understand grief, how to work through it, and how to help people move back into their lives with a sense of meaning.

"You are not alone" goes both ways, though. You may find that healing doesn't just happen by receiving—sometimes, more healing can happen in the giving. Even if you're in the depths of your suffering right now, it may be hard to think about you being further down the road and some other kid following up behind you. As you move up this trail toward healing and wholeness, you may eventually find that you're the experienced guide, that you're the one who can help somebody else find their way. And it feels good when that happens. That "not-aloneness" can go both ways.

Most of our friends have found meaning and purpose in being able to take the things they've learned on their grief journeys and being able to pay those gifts forward. Some of those acts of kindness and empathy might take place in organized grief support groups, where they, as the older, more experienced teens, can have the chance to throw an arm around a newcomer. They can tell that new kid whose grief might be very fresh and raw that "I know it hurts. But you're here now. And it can get better."

GRACE

Grace has some experience helping other kids feel welcomed and understood. "I'm just thirteen, but I've been around this for a while," she said. "When new kids come in, a lot of times they're mostly shy and don't ask a lot of questions. Maybe they'll say their name, but just keep quiet after that. If there's a new girl, I'll try to show her that she's around us kids who understand. I'll start by just saying, 'I'm sorry'—not 'I'm sorry for your loss,' but just 'I'm sorry.' There's a difference between the two.

"I might ask if I can give her a hug," Grace said. "I might ask her about some good memory she has of her person. I want to show kids that even if we're not a biological family, we're a family we've made here in our group. I try to be the person who can tell them, 'Hey . . . it's okay. I promise that it gets better.' If they can feel your love, they might look up to you as someone who's lived it. I hope a new kid could say to herself, 'Well, Grace has been there, and she says it'll get better. So maybe I will feel okay.'"

JDB

JDB has also been going to his support groups for several years. As he's grown and carried his memories of his dad into his midteenage years, he finds that he too has something to give back. "When the older kids left for college, that left me in the upper age range for kids in my group. It's sad when the older kids leave because it's like family members are moving out. We just got a new group of kids to join our group. They vary from age thirteen up to high school seniors. I try to give them the best support I can because that's what was given to me. I've been around long enough that I can tell them, 'You've found a group now. Keep coming. Don't give up if you think things aren't changing fast enough. It's not going to happen immediately, but things do get better. Just keep coming.'"

The lessons of empathy and the gifts of patience that you can find in support groups sometimes get paid forward in unexpected ways. Dexter talked about a time after his dad died that one of his friends wasn't being very understanding and even a little judgmental. Dexter said that he understood how friends sometimes just can't relate to losing someone they love if they haven't been through it themselves. But not long after that, "my friend lost his father due to some medical reason," Dexter said. "I gave him a call and said I hoped he was doing okay. My friend told me, 'Now I understand how you feel.' I told him about my group meetings at the Dougy Center, and if he needed people to talk to, this might be a help. I'm still checking in on him and trying to let him know he'll always have friends he can lean on."

The healing you can personally find in helping others isn't limited to just welcoming or mentoring younger kids in support groups.

KATE

Kate tells a story about being on vacation with her family when she was about six. They came across a man who looked like he might have been homeless and maybe on drugs. He was trying to get a bus home but didn't have enough money for the fare. "My dad told the guy he'd pay for his bus ticket," Kate said, "as long as he promised to get himself some help. This guy started bawling. He hugged my dad and said that no one had ever helped him like that before. I always remembered that, and I had a chance to use it years later." Kate continued and told about a man who used to work at her high school. He had lost his job and ended up homeless. Kate saw him out walking and invited him to sit in a coffee shop with her. "I remembered what I had seen my father do, and I wanted to live up to his example. I got the man something to eat and talked with him for a couple of hours," Kate said. "He had no money, so I gave him $60 and told him I hoped he was able to find a job and get back on his feet. I was a freshman in college and had little money myself. But I told him to take it because he needed it more than I did. He just cried. It made me feel so much better about my day, hoping I'd made a difference for him."

Reaching outside of yourself to do something kind for other people can be a great way to change your perspective and may help you get unstuck if you're feeling stuck. There's an inevitable lightening of the darkness when you do something kind or generous or thoughtful for another person. You'll feel that lightness when you hear a "thank-you" from a homeless man to whom you've just served lunch in a homeless shelter. You'll feel it when you visit a nursing home and read to a resident from her favorite novel, and you see a gentle smile on her face as she remembers the story she might have first heard as a teen about your age.

It doesn't even have to be human beings you're reaching out to help. Volunteering at a Humane Society or other animal shelter is a great way to brighten a day. Grace found plenty of comfort with animals. "If you're sad, you know what makes you feel better?" she said. "Dogs! If you're sad, you can sit there and pet a dog for a long time. It really helps."

If you want to reach outside of yourself to do something thoughtful for another person, you can find plenty of great ideas. That kindness doesn't have to be a big production, and you can even be anonymous when you do it. Here are a few ideas:

- Pick up the tab for the person behind you in the Starbucks drive-through.

- Take a bag with you when you walk a trail so that you can pick up stray wrappers or empty bottles left by others.

- If your person took their own life, volunteer for a suicide prevention hotline.

- Drop a quarter in somebody's parking meter if you see their time is running out.

- If you have an older neighbor, cut their grass or rake their leaves or shovel their driveway, without telling them.

- If your person died of a heart attack, help raise money for research by joining in an American Heart Association Heart Walk.

- Send a text to a friend at random and tell them something you appreciate about them.

- Give up your seat to someone who is standing.

- Find another kid who is suffering through their grief, and sit and listen to them.

- If you see kids selling lemonade in their front yard, buy some.

Reaching out and helping someone else can be a good way to feel better about where you are. It can return some of your power to you when you might be feeling powerless. It can change and brighten your outlook to know that another person's day gets better because of something you did.

We can also reach out to help other people by the example we show in how we carry ourselves in the face of our loss. It's a deep truth that all of us who allow ourselves to love will eventually experience the sadness and grief of losing a person we love. We break up, somebody leaves, somebody dies.

When that grief comes upon us, don't we look around to other people for examples of how they suffered grief and still lived through it? How did they bear up under the inconceivable death of a best friend, or a sibling, or a parent? What did they do to endure and keep living? What examples can we find in the strength of others? Carrying those questions a step further, when other teens follow behind us and are experiencing their grief, will we be an example of strength to them?

Do you know the story about the Battle of Thermopylae in 480 BC? Several thousand Greek soldiers and three hundred Spartan warriors assembled at a narrow coastal pass called Thermopylae (which means "the hot gates" for the natural hot springs that flowed from the rocks there). Their mission was to hold back the invading Persian army long enough to give the rest of the Greek city-states time to prepare a defense. (The movie *300* was based on this historical battle.)

The Greeks were outnumbered at Thermopylae. There wasn't any hope of a military victory, and they all knew it. They didn't expect to live and hoped only that their valor and bravery would inspire the feuding Greek city-states to come together as one. The Spartans knew that the only way the Greek civilization could all survive was if they stood together—and not alone.

In his historical novel about the battle, *Gates of Fire*, author Steven Pressfield writes a scene where the Spartan king Leonidas is talking to the lady Paraleia, whose husband and son have both been picked as warriors who will go to fight and certainly die at the hot gates. Leonidas wants to share with this bereaved mother and wife why he has chosen her son and her husband. Leonidas tells Paraleia that he selected which Spartan warriors would go to Thermopylae, not because of their strength, swiftness, or valor in previous battles. He picked them based on the strength of the women in their families. Leonidas says:

> When the battle is over when the Three Hundred have gone down
> to death, then will all Greece look to the Spartans, to see how they

bear it. But who, lady, who will the Spartans look to? To you. To you and the other wives and mothers, sisters and daughters of the fallen.

If they behold your hearts riven and broken with grief, they, too, will break. And Greece will break with them. But if you bear up, dry-eyed, not alone enduring your loss but seizing it with contempt for its agony and embracing it as the honor that it is in truth, then Sparta will stand. And all [Greece] will stand behind her.

What does a story from 480 BC have to do with us today? It's that "we're not alone." People all around us are living examples that it is possible to experience the death of someone we love, to bear it up, to be able to heal and to live forward with meaning and purpose. We have only to look around to find them.

The sisters and mothers and wives of Sparta can be an example for all of us. They can embody an example of hope for what your future may hold. And in that future, you may end up being the one to whom other teenagers look for an example of healing and meaning. Other kids may look to you for ideas of how you were able to bear your loss and maybe follow your example of hope and strength. You may find a sense of peace and strength in being able to help other kids down a path you've fought bravely to travel yourself. It could be one of those things that can help you find meaning in the journey you're on.

CHAPTER TWELVE

TAKING CARE OF YOUR BODY

When we experience the death of someone we love, we don't just feel that pain in our minds and our emotions and our hearts. It's suffering we feel in our bodies too. You probably know the feeling of being anxious, and having your stomach feel queasy or knotted up. When you feel fearful or sad, you may recognize a feeling of being deflated or drained or having a sense of great heaviness.

Some people think our minds and our bodies are two different things, as if the mind is a small bus driver behind our eyes, telling our bodies where to go and what to do. Other people feel like body and mind are one thing and just different reflections of that same one thing.

Either way you look at it, taking good care of your body as you go through the grieving process can give you strength and resilience. Having a strong and rested body can make it easier to get up in the morning and face what comes next. It can help you keep a clear mind and give you some calm and focus.

EATING WELL

When you're grieving, your eating patterns can tend to get messed up. Some kids find that feelings of sadness can put a damper on their appetite. Some may just forget to eat, or others might even feel like they're turning away from food to deny themselves any pleasure at all.

Other teens may find solace in overeating. There's a good reason why rich and filling dishes like mac and cheese, biscuits and gravy, or meat loaf are called "comfort foods." If we feel like we have an empty space within us, isn't warm banana-nut bread or a plate of chocolate chip cookies a good way to fill that space and make us feel less sad? You bet. Sometimes we might eat just because we're bored or don't want to think about loss anymore—and throwing a blanket of pancakes over the top of those feelings seems like as good a way as any to keep from feeling them.

On the other hand, plenty of good reasons exist to be intentional about what we're eating, and even to use mealtime in a practice of mindfulness. Picking the right foods and being aware of how you're eating them can help you avoid the lethargy of feeling overfed. By eating well and choosing healthy foods to fuel yourself, you can bolster your mood and help maintain a stable self-image.

If you can, steer away from processed or prepared food that might come out of cans or boxes, and opt for real food: veggies and fruits, greens and salads, lean proteins like chicken or fish or tofu. Nuts and berries are good choices; they're kind of like nature's candy. Try switching from sugary soft drinks, and keep yourself well hydrated with cool, clear water.

Sometimes it's easy to settle in front of the television or YouTube to binge-watch shows or videos and have a stack of snacks at hand to keep you company. We've all done it. But before you know it, you've gone through half a season of *The Office* reruns and a whole bag of tortilla chips.

You might try something called "mindful eating." It can be part of your meditation practice, with the object of your awareness being the food on your plate (rather than feeling the sensations of your breath). To practice mindful eating, leave any distractions aside. Put down your phone, put down your iPad, and turn off the TV. Don't worry; it doesn't have to be for a long time—twenty minutes should do. Instagram will be there when you're finished.

Make yourself a plate. Sit down at the table, but don't dive right in. Take a moment to appreciate the different colors and textures of the food in front of you: fresh green spinach leaves and cream cheese on a soft tortilla wrap; crisp slices of sweet red pepper, cold and crunchy; a handful of fat, red grapes.

Imagine for a moment the spinach growing out of rich, dark earth, its leaves receiving the sunlight. Think of the calloused hands of the farmworker sorting through the grapes—the truck driver who delivered it all to your local grocery. As you take each bite, you might think of it almost as if it were a sacrament—a gift of life from the world to you. Chew slowly, deliberately. Have an awareness of how the tortilla tears as you bite it, and how it embraces the creamy texture of the cheese, paired with the leafy crunch of the spinach. Take a grape (one at a time, please!) and feel the happy burst of sweetness as it pops between your teeth. As you swallow, picture your belly filling with this nourishing chow that you're not just "eating" but are now "experiencing."

If you give mindful eating a try, you may find that you eat less, enjoy it more, and discover that you have a relationship with your food—which could be good for your body, as well as for your mind and spirit.

Having said this, don't deny yourself a relationship with a slice of pizza or a bowl of ice cream on occasion. That can be good for your spirit too.

GETTING GOOD SLEEP

Getting good sleep is important to help us function in the world, especially when we're under a lot of stress. They say we need about eight hours of sleep per night. When you total it up, that comes out to almost three thousand hours of sleep every year. If we need that much sleep, it must be pretty important. If we're not getting enough sleep or the quality of our sleep is poor, that can make it harder to keep a clear mind and strong body and do what we need to do in going forward in the midst of loss and grief.

Consistent nights of uninterrupted sleep can help you stay strong in a lot of ways. Deep sleep is when many of the day's memories are consolidated, so it can help you retain more of what you learn in school. Being well rested can make you more clear headed during the day and have improved judgment. Not getting enough sleep (called "sleep

deprivation") can slow you down during the day and can even contrib-
ute to depression and weight gain.

Grief can disrupt our sleep patterns. And just like everything else
about the grieving process, not everybody responds the same way. Some
teens start sleeping more than they had before. You may wake up in the
morning and want to do nothing but pull the covers over your head and
never get out of bed again. Mourning the death of your person is hard
and can take a lot of energy out of you. No wonder you feel tired. Sleep
can be an escape—that time when you can close your eyes and drift
away and not have to think about how much you miss your person.

Or it can go the other way. Some kids find that they have insomnia,
like there's a movie running in their heads that they have trouble turning
off. Who can sleep with a movie running through their heads? Other
kids might even avoid sleep because they want to avoid the dreams or
nightmares that come in the dark.

The Dalai Lama was noted to say that "sleep is the best meditation." Since meditation is something you "practice," you can improve
the quality of your sleep with some simple practices like these:

- Cut down on the caffeinated drinks earlier in your day. Half of the
  caffeine from your coffee or soft drink is still in your system up to
  five hours later.

- Pick a bedtime routine and try to hit the sheets at the same time
  every night—even on the weekend. Our bodies respond well to
  that kind of consistency.

- Turn off your screens (phones, tablets, computers, TV) an hour or
  two before it's time to lie down. The light from electronics can fake
  out your body clock and make your body think it's earlier in the
  day and can make it harder to fall into a good sleep.

- Find some calming activities to relax your body and mind before
  bed, maybe doing meditation or deep breathing exercises. Or pick
  up a good book.

- Eat and drink lightly in the evening.

- Make sure your room is dark and cool. Minimize disruptions and put on some comfortable pajamas or sweats.

- If you wake up during the night, you don't have to lie there and fret about not sleeping. Get up, find a comfortable chair, and read a book or write in your journal until you feel sleepy enough to lie down again.

A third of your life is meant for sleeping. So the better your sleep, the better you'll be able to sort through all the challenges of that life. In his popular novel *The Perks of Being a Wallflower*, novelist Stephen Chbosky writes: "Put my head under my pillow, and let the quiet put things where they are supposed to be."

GETTING PHYSICAL

We can find plenty of examples of how our bodies and our emotions are connected. You probably know the feeling of getting bad news and then feeling dizzy or having your stomach clench up. You've probably also experienced a "tingle run up your spine" when listening to some exhilarating and soaring piece of music you love, or maybe when you walk through a door and have your friends yell, "Surprise!!" for a little happy birthday ambush.

Our bodies don't just respond to passing emotions—they can also hold on to those emotions and become a storehouse of anxiety and sadness and grief. Can you relate to this? Do you feel like you're "carrying a weight" or feel a stiffness in your back or neck? Maybe a dull headache that seems to persist? Or just an overall feeling of fatigue and tiredness? Feelings of grief can cause inflammation in parts of your body and can tamp down your immune system and make you more susceptible to getting sick.

Getting your body moving with exercise and physical activity can help get those emotions moving and help strengthen you and keep you from getting sick too. It's not that exercise will make your grief go away, but it can help keep all that sadness from taking up residence in your back or your neck or your belly. Any kind of exercise will do: a walk or run or maybe a session of yoga by yourself or in a class. You can find YouTube channels with yoga sessions, like the channel Yoga with Adriene.

Getting your body moving through dance can help. Author and novelist Elizabeth Gilbert talked with life coach Marie Forleo about her experiences after losing her partner Rayya Elias to cancer. Gilbert spoke about what her grief felt like, and how getting physically active—especially dancing—helped as she worked with her feelings. She said: "Grief is a heavy cement that gets into your bones and pulls you down. Dance is the way of letting energy move through you so it can move out of you."

Getting yourself moving with dance, running, weight training, spinning classes, or swimming can help your body pump out those neurotransmitters like serotonin and endorphins (responsible for that euphoric "runner's high" you may have heard about). Exercise can help fend off feelings of depression or can simply make you feel better about yourself walking around in a now-fit body.

Other physical activities, like hitting punching bags, can help you vent feelings of anger or frustration in a way that doesn't hurt yourself or others. Many grief counseling centers for young people, like the Dougy Center in Portland, Oregon, or Brooke's Place in Indianapolis, Indiana, have rooms for kids and teens they call "the volcano room." Hit on punching bags, whack the walls with a foam baton, or just simply let it out. Getting those hot emotions moving can make sure they don't sit and smolder and can make room for other, cooler, emotions.

GRACE

Grace found that the "volcano room" at Brooke's Place helped her a lot. "They have old phone books that you can rip up," she said.

"You can scream if you want. If I have a bad day, a good scream helps sometimes. The room is soundproofed . . . mostly," Grace said and then laughed to herself. "They have those foam pool noodles that you can hit against the wall, or beanbags you can hit. The volcano room is good because you can work out some of your pain without physical fighting."

BAILEY

Bailey said that being physically active with her friends helped her a lot. "I found that playing volleyball helps me feel good. When I'm on the court and playing volleyball, I'm not thinking about any of the pain that I have," she said. "I also like working out and gaming. 'Magic: The Gathering' is fun, and helps me get out with people and doing activities. Generally, when I'm being productive and have something to do, I feel good, and I'm fairly happy."

LOGAN

Having safe and productive ways to deal with the conflicting emotions of grief can be important. Some of our friends had to learn the hard way. Logan had a tough time with anger after his dad died. He said, "I wasn't dealing with my dad's death very well, and I would get my anger out in a physical way—and maybe not the best way. For a while there, I was putting my fists through the walls and doors. I know I caused a lot of damage. After a while, I was able to find better ways to deal with my anger, like being outdoors and in the woods. I also learned that working on a project in the garage and just keeping my hands and mind busy, that relaxed me a lot," he said. "Sometimes, it was just as helpful to go into my room and get on the phone with a close friend or one of my dad's buddies."

JDB

Getting physical can have benefits that go beyond improving one's mood or health benefits or feeling more fit and toned. Sports had been a big part of JDB's relationship with his dad. "I played football, basketball, and baseball," he said, "and my dad was usually the coach or involved with the team somehow." JDB's dad got him involved in martial arts, and he found that the practice of tae kwon do brought him more gifts than just being able to defend himself or break a board with a roundhouse kick. "I had worked my way up almost to second-degree black belt in tae kwon do," JDB said. "I think my practice in martial arts helped grow my sense of patience. I also gained some ability to be able to look at things with a sense of perspective. I'd see how some friends in my support group could be pessimistic, and others more optimistic. I decided that I wanted to be as optimistic as I could because it just helps to live that way." Beyond the physical benefits or sense of perspective he gained from practicing tae kwon do, JDB added, "I gained a lot of good friends out of martial arts." From his practice of tae kwon do, JDB might have also found some truth and perspective in the words of the famed martial artist and philosopher Bruce Lee: "Do not wish for an easy life. Wish for the strength to endure a difficult one."

GETTING OUTSIDE INTO NATURE

The Japanese call it *shinrin-yoku* or "immersing oneself in the forest" or just "forest bathing." It's an artful way of saying "taking a walk outside." Put your phone in your pocket. Slow down. Immerse yourself in the natural world and take time to notice things you may otherwise have missed if you were Snapchatting or checking Instagram.

Notice the way a cloud changes shape, in slow motion. Follow a bee making its rounds, visiting the clover in a neighbor's yard or the coneflower along a wooded trail. Tune into the babble of water in a brook that runs to a river that runs to a sea. Hear a *skritch-skritch* from a high tree branch, and find a squirrel chewing its way into the meaty heart of a walnut. Just be outside and take time to notice it all.

When you're carrying a heavy burden of grief, what good is it, you might ask, being in nature and paying attention to bees and squirrels?

Is it anything more than just a pleasant change of scenery? Yes, actually. Science has spent some time studying the benefits we gain from spending time outside. Going outdoors can reduce stress and anxiety, reduce fatigue, and help you focus. It can lift your mood and help you feel calmer and even boost your immune function. All these benefits can bring a degree of healing—physically and mentally and emotionally— which are all good to have in your pocket when you're working with the grief of losing someone you love. And it's not a huge time commitment either; going outside twenty minutes a day can do it. You can go longer, of course, but you don't have to get all Jeremiah Johnson or Bear Grylls about it. Just go for a walk or a hike.

How does being outside in nature help improve your mood? Theories abound: sunlight gives us a boost of vitamin D; the scent of pine or lilac is like free aromatherapy; the peace and quiet of being on a wooded trail can reduce the stress hormone cortisol. Sounds sciency, doesn't it? WebMD even has a page on "ecotherapy." Here's another way to think about being outside in nature.

Modern humans (that's us) have been around for about three hundred thousand years. Cities, on the other hand, didn't show up in Mesopotamia until maybe seven thousand years ago. For most of our collective history, we've lived outside: feeling the wind, seeing the stars unobscured by the lights of shopping malls, feeling the coming and going of the seasons. We didn't evolve to live in cities—we evolved to be outdoors. We're built and wired for it. Our bodies respond to being outside. Maybe the reason that our mood improves and that we feel calmer when we're out in nature is that our bodies are recognizing that "being in nature means coming home."

As we look at how the outdoors can help work through the pain and longing of grief, we can take it one more step. Try this and see how it feels: We're not "on the earth" or "in nature," as if we parachuted in here from somewhere else. We are "of the earth" and "of nature." We grew out of the earth, along with all other living things. We reunite with them when we go into a woods, onto a river, or down a trail in a city park. Some outdoor enthusiasts talk about how "we're part of the earth, rather than apart from it."

We're so much a part of nature that we can map a "cousin rela-tionship" to every living being on earth. The website Evogeneao.com lets you play with an interactive Tree of Life (in English or Spanish). It shows you the whole tree—from four billion years ago to the pres-ent. You can click to show the relationships between "family members." Humans and horses? We're 21 millionth cousins, 47 million times removed. People and flowering plants? Try 2.9 billionth cousins, 1.8 billion times removed.

You and nature are part of one thing. When you're out in the world, on the water, under the trees, among the animals of the land and the air, you are among your family. Going into nature to "find yourself" is more than just a metaphor.

There's plenty of range to roam if you want to get out and into nature. In the U.S., federal public lands like national parks and national forests offer 640 million acres where we're all free to hike, mountain bike, canoe, and camp. State parks around the U.S. number about 6,600, offering another fourteen million acres where you can get your boots dirty and your spirits clean. Closer to home for a lot of people, city parks around the country cover about twelve million acres, to say nothing of county parks, neighborhood trails, or munic-ipal bike paths.

KATE

Kate found that water, wind, and sun helped her spirit. "I've learned that a long bike ride helps me. I'll ride along Lake Michi-gan, maybe twenty-five miles total. I'll listen to music while I ride. Just tune things out and look at the world around me," she said. "Aren't we kind of stuck in this world where our minds are con-stantly running, always thinking? For me, getting on my bike and being outside and riding is a way of quieting all that noise."

LOGAN

For Logan, time in the wilderness appeals to him more than a lakeside bike ride. "Being in the outdoors, hunting and fishing is something I like," Logan said. "The area behind my house in Oregon is wooded and secluded. My buddies will come over, and we'll set up practice targets to get ready for hunting season. I've hunted pretty much everything: elk, deer, even black bear and mountain lion. My dad has a lot of military friends, one who was a Green Beret, and I'll go fishing and hunting with them, too. That's when I get to hear some of their stories about my dad. Whether it's crazy party stories or their Redwood Run motorcycle stories—I love hearing stories of my dad as just a normal guy. It makes me remember him as more human. I find that's my favorite time, being in the outdoors with my dad's friends." Being outside and being a hunter has given Logan some insights about living too. Logan said, "I like a hunting show called *MeatEater*, with this guy Steven Rinella. You can see from his shows that hunting means being prepared and being patient. And I like that he's not afraid to show that, in hunting, sometimes you're going to come away unsuccessful. There are some good life lessons in all that."

GRACE

Grace keeps it simple—no bicycle, no camouflage jacket, just her and her pup. "If I get upset, sometimes I'll take the dog out on a walk," she said. "That way, he can get some exercise, and I can get out of the house to get some fresh air, which helps me calm down and clear my head."

DEXTER

Dexter appreciates the outdoors, too, and finds comfort out there. "It helps me to be outside," he said. "It can be as little as going for a walk or throwing a football with a friend or playing a game of baseball. It kind of mediates my stress just to know I can be outside on a nice day, and that I can just breathe."

As you keep on moving forward into life, grief can get heavy. Being in the outdoors can let some sunlight wash over that grief. Outside, the winds can fill your sails and help pull you along when you're feeling stuck in the water. Outdoors, you could start a garden, and take up a fistful of warm soil and squeeze a little bit of your grief into it. Return that soil to the earth and see if it doesn't carry off a bit of that grief for you, so you don't have to carry it all yourself (and maybe it'll help grow something beautiful).

Nature offers us its gifts of reconnection and healing. English poet William Blake knew something about the benefits of being close to the land and finding gifts that one won't find on crowded urban boulevards. His poem "Gnomic Verses" says it well: "Great things are done when men and mountains meet / This is not done by jostling in the street."

CHAPTER THIRTEEN

TAKING CARE OF RELATIONSHIPS

O ur relationships define us. When somebody asks, "Who are you?" isn't your first answer usually something about who you are in relation to somebody else? "I'm Charlie's brother" or "I'm Claire's friend" or "I'm Madelyn's daughter."

Our last names often show how we're interrelated: if you're a Johnson, you're a "son of John." If you're of Irish or Scottish descent, you might have the last name of O'Connor ("I'm descended from Connor") or MacGregor ("I'm a child of Gregor"). Spanish surnames add "ez" or "az" to a father's name: "Maria Alvarez" would be "Maria, daughter of Alvaro."

Sometimes our surnames show our connections with the world by naming the roles in which our ancestors served each other. People with last names like Baker or Fisher or Hunter provided food to the tribe. Masons and Carpenters and Wrights built each other's shelters. Zapateros made shoes, and Guerreros were soldiers.

We exist in these webs of relationships where we've descended from each other and serve each other. When somebody we love dies, it hurts. We miss them—we miss their faces, their laughter, their practical jokes. We miss their company and how they listened intently when we'd tell a story. You miss those private memories that only you and your person shared, and you miss the memories that you won't have the opportunity to create next month or next year.

When someone we love dies, we're losing not only that person, but we're also losing a part of ourselves. You might have said, "I feel an empty space inside" or "I feel like a part of me is missing." We are so defined by our relationships with the people we love; when they die, a part of us is lost too. If your mother dies, that part of yourself that is "your mother's daughter" is now missing. When your friend Kyle dies, that part of you that was "Kyle's best friend" goes away too.

Our relationships and connections with others can also serve us in our time of need. While relationships can sometimes be a source of friction, the bonds we feel with our friends and family can be a source of strength and support as we work with feelings of grief.

TOGETHER OR ALONE

The spiritual teacher Ram Dass liked to say, "We are all just walking each other home." It's a good way to look at these life journeys: we're all walking a path, and we don't have to do it alone. Togetherness is good, and being in the company of people who understand and support you can help lessen the burden of carrying all your grief by yourself. At the same time, solitude can be a healing experience. Gladly, we don't have to choose between one over the other. You can choose solitude or camaraderie, or you can have both—on your terms.

Kahlil Gibran was a Lebanese American poet who lived from 1883 to 1931. He wrote a great poem about how we can balance our desires for solitude with our need to be with others who love us and whom we love. If you've attended weddings, you might have heard Gibran's poem "On Marriage" being read as part of the ceremony (from his collection called *The Prophet*). While this poem speaks to people getting ready to join their lives in marriage, the theme of "togetherness versus solitude" applies to those of us who are working through grief. We are trying to find a balance between wanting to be alone sometimes, and wanting the comfort of being around other people with whom we have bonds of affection and love. "On Marriage" goes like this:

Then Almitra spoke again and said, And what of Marriage, master?
And he answered saying: You were born together,
and together you shall be forevermore.

You shall be together when the white wings of death scatter your days.
Ay, you shall be together even in the silent memory of God.
But let there be spaces in your togetherness,
And let the winds of the heavens dance between you.

Love one another, but make not a bond of love:
Let it rather be a moving sea between the shores of your souls.
Fill each other's cup but drink not from one cup.
Give one another of your bread but eat not from the same loaf.
Sing and dance together and be joyous,
but let each one of you be alone,
Even as the strings of a lute are alone though
they quiver with the same music.

Give your hearts, but not into each other's keeping.
For only the hand of Life can contain your hearts.
And stand together yet not too near together:
For the pillars of the temple stand apart,
And the oak tree and the cypress grow not in each other's shadow.

This idea of aloneness and togetherness as strings of an instrument quivering with the same music would also seem to resonate with our friends. Many of them found that they needed alone time just as much as they needed the warm embrace of their friends, and of others who understood and cared about them.

GRACE

Grace places a lot of value on being able to make her own choices about whether or not to join in support group discussions at Brooke's Place. "One of the things I like about my group is that they always let us talk when we need to. If I want to opt out of group talk, I can," Grace said. "Or if I feel like I want to talk one-on-one with a counselor or a volunteer, I can do that. I like having it be up to me. If I'm sad at that moment, I don't have to do what everyone else is doing. I can just take those moments to be sad."

KATE

Kate likes her alone time, for sure. But she's also very social and finds a lot of comfort being around the people she loves. "They say that for a person in prison, solitary confinement is the worst punishment there is. You get stuck inside yourself," Kate said. "We find our humanity in our relationships. If you're always alone, you can lose your humanity. I feel like, without deep connections to other people, you're not going to be able to heal."

BAILEY

Being alone is hard for Bailey, but she also finds it hard to be around people. It's difficult to find the balance, she said. "I found myself not wanting to be alone, just because I didn't want to think about my sister, which always happened when I was alone and didn't have anything to distract me," Bailey said. "But it was also hard to reach out and be around people because it's difficult to share these feelings with others. They don't know how I'm feeling and what's going on, and I feel vulnerable just thinking about trying to tell other people how I feel, which is why even today, I've never really talked about it."

JDB

Others of our friends, like JDB, find it easier to strike a balance. He said, "I think I'm good at gauging how much time I spend surrounding myself with other people, but then making time to spend with myself." He said that he doesn't feel like making time for himself is shutting himself off or feeling sorry for himself. "I just enjoy being alone sometimes," he said.

As you're sorting through your grief, you should feel empowered to make your own choices about how you divide your time between solitude and togetherness with those around you. You need both, and only you can decide how much togetherness and how much alone time is right for you.

Author David Kessler has written many times that "grief has to be witnessed." It's in togetherness, with the right friends, where your grief can be witnessed, and where the people you love can acknowledge your pain. In doing so, they can take just a little bit of that weight from your shoulders, so you don't have to carry it all by yourself.

Writer and conservationist Terry Tempest Williams talked about not being afraid to bear witness to sorrow. In her conversation on the *Insights at the Edge* podcast with Tami Simon, Terry said, "I am not married to sorrow. I just choose not to look away. And I think there is deep beauty in not averting our gaze. No matter how hard it is, no matter how heart-breaking it can be. It is about presence. It is about bearing witness. I used to think bearing witness was a passive act. I don't believe that anymore. I think that when we are present, when we bear witness, when we do not divert our gaze, something is revealed—the very marrow of life. We change. A transformation occurs. Our consciousness shifts."

With the right support, whether in grief support groups or with trusted friends, having our grief witnessed can make transformation happen—both in others and in ourselves.

Yet still, the quiet call of solitude can offer the comfort that cannot be found among other people. In her book *Why I Wake Early*, Pulitzer Prize–winning poet Mary Oliver spoke of this in her verse "The Old Poets of China":

> Wherever I am, the world comes after me.
> It offers me its busyness. It does not believe
> that I do not want it. Now I understand
> why the old poets of China went so far and high
> into the mountains, then crept into the pale mist

Solitude can be found high in those mountains in that pale mist, but the value of solitude is not only in holding us apart from others. In his book *Warrior of the Light*, Brazilian novelist Paulo Coelho writes about how solitude and relationship are two sides of the same coin. He writes that just as fire teaches us about water, anger shows us the value of peace, and death shows us the value of life, solitude teaches us how to live with other people.

RELATING WITH YOUR FRIENDS

Going through a life-changing experience like having a parent die, or a brother or sister, or a best friend, can change a lot of things in how we think about ourselves and can change our relationships. Sometimes those changes in us and our friends can bring us closer together, but sometimes they can drive a wedge between us too. Having a sense of patience, and even forgiveness, can be helpful when relating to friends as both they and you figure out how to relate to each other as you go through the process of grieving.

Our friends had a lot to say about how the people in their circles were a source of support to them. They also talked about challenges that come with trying to help their friends understand what it's like for them to be in grief. It seems to be extra hard for our friends whose person died because of violence or suicide.

BAILEY

Bailey has a good understanding of these challenges and how to relate with compassion to her friends. "I feel like everyone recognized that my sister taking her own life was a sensitive topic. When we talked, most of them censored themselves and tried to avoid saying anything that could bring Sydney into a conversation. Some of my friends simply just didn't know what to say or how to act because they'd never been through that kind of loss before," Bailey said. "They might think they're doing you a favor by not bringing it up because they think if they say something, it might bring you pain. They don't know how grief feels, and they can't figure out a way to interact with you," she said. "All of that can be okay if you can be understanding that they're just unsure of how to handle your situation, and they're doing their best." Bailey continued, "If I could go back, I wish I would've been more vocal and open to my friends about what I was feeling and what I needed from them to help get me through this. Sometimes, I feel like I turned away from my friends because it's just so hard to open up and say what you need."

GRACE

Grace had some similar experiences with her friends being unsure about how to relate to her grief in losing her dad at such a young age. "Sometimes, it's hard talking about how I'm feeling with my friends because no one wants to talk about it," Grace said. "If I'd say something about my dad, they might just say, 'Oh,' and then move on. I understand that some people don't want to be awkward, or don't want to hurt somebody's feelings and get them all crying by mentioning a sensitive topic like a parent dying. So they kind of shut down and avoid talking with me about it at all," she said.

KATE

When Kate's mom died from circumstances related to violence and drug addiction, she was afraid that her friends would judge her. "I don't fear a lot of things, but sometimes I feared that people would think of me differently because of what our family went through. They might say, 'My God, she's been through all this? Maybe she's going to have problems.'" Through both the hard work of counseling and a lot of personal introspection, Kate has been able to gain perspectives on the experience of losing her mom to violence. "I'm able to see that this is one chapter in my life. It's part of my story, but it's not the whole story of the human I am. I feel like if you're confident knowing that, you can be less afraid about what people think of you," Kate said. Over time, Kate has been able to develop a sense of empathy and understanding for her friends. "Sometimes, friends aren't going to know how to react to you losing someone so important in your life, especially if they've never lost someone. It takes emotional maturity to genuinely feel what you're feeling for them to step back and say, 'I'm sorry, how can I help you?' I wanted to be able to tell them that I felt insecure and scared because I just lost this important person my life. I wanted to tell them I appreciated that they were there for me. I wanted to let them know that I'm not broken. I wanted them to understand how I was working through my experience, and that I'd get back to myself at some point. Mostly I wanted to let them know that I'm thankful to have them as friends."

JDB

In JDB's experience, his close friends have given him a lot of support, even if his reliance on friends has caused a bit of friction. "My mom's big on family," JDB said. "She says blood family will always be more important than friends. That's an area where we kind of knock heads, because sometimes I think that friends can become like family, too." He spoke about how his many friends have included a core group of about five kids who are his closest friends. "They're the ones I feel like I can share the details with," JDB said. "Sometimes they didn't say much or ask much like they didn't want to pry. But they know me and know my situation. They're the ones who I can talk to about what's going on and how I'm feeling about my dad dying. They get me, even though a lot of them hadn't had deaths in their own families. To tell the truth, being able to let your friends get close is just nice . . . it's so much better than being alone."

LOGAN

Friends can sometimes represent a risk, too, depending on what kind of foundation those friendships are built. Logan had a rough time in the months after his dad died, and he said that it took him a while to figure things out. "Freshman year, I got mixed up with the wrong people—drinking and doing drugs and partying a lot," Logan said. "After I did that for a bit, I realized that this was only making things worse. It wasn't helping with any kind of healing, and it was making the process of forgiving take a lot longer. I slowly cut back on the drinking and the smoking," he said. "Once I stopped all that, I found that a lot of those partying 'friends' kind of disappeared, which says something. I ended up getting closer to my best friend and my dad's buddies. If there's something I'd want other kids to know from my story, it would be this: you're not going to find much going down a road of trying to fix your feelings through partying. I can tell you from experience that it doesn't help."

KATE

Kate talked about the great surprise of having her relationships enriched in unexpected and fulfilling ways. "I think that if we take the time to open ourselves up and allow ourselves to be vulnerable, that vulnerability helps build connections that can be lifelong," she said. "At the same time, that shared opening helps the other person also to feel more comfortable in sharing their stories with you. All that builds a stronger bond between people in ways you'd never expect. They will be there for you and go through so many things with you. Being able to support each other through grief and all the other hard things that life gives us, it's a way to find out who your true friends are. And once you know who they are, you know they're with you forever."

LOGAN

Logan would agree and talked about a fast friendship he made through his involvement in group support meetings at the Dougy Center near his home in Portland, Oregon. "The sessions there have been very, very helpful to me," Logan said. "I actually made a very close friendship there. Like me, he also lost his father to a heart attack. We found we have similar interests, and we've gone hunting together. We've spent a lot of time together both at the Dougy Center and outside of it. I'd say I'm lucky to find a friend like that."

DEALING WITH WELL-MEANING ADVICE

Even as far back as ancient Rome, people were trying to figure out how to talk to each other about grief. You can see that struggle in a letter the Stoic philosopher Seneca sent to his mother, Helvia. Her mother died giving birth to her. Helvia had lost her husband and had grandchildren die in her arms, including Seneca's only son. When Seneca was later banished from Rome, Helvia was carrying a lot of grief.

From his exile in Corsica, Seneca's letter reflected his struggle to find the right words to share with his grieving mother. He wrote:

> I have often had the urge to console you and often restrained it. First, I thought I would be laying aside all my troubles when I had at least wiped away your tears, even if I could not stop them coming. I realized that your grief should not be intruded upon while it was fresh and agonizing, in case the consolations themselves should rouse and inflame it: for an illness too, nothing is more harmful than premature treatment. So I was waiting until your grief of itself should lose its force and, being softened by time to endure remedies, it would allow itself to be touched and handled.

Even two thousand years later, people today have the same struggles. It's hard to know the right thing to say or when to say it. You may see your friends or adults in your life struggling with trying to find words of comfort or wisdom or perspective to offer you. They mean well, but you may have had things like this said to you:

- "It was God's will."

- "Everything happens for a reason."

- "You'll see them again."

- "They'll always be with you."

- "Look at the positives."

- "At least you still have your other parent."

- "You'll get over it."

Words like these probably don't help much, do they? One way to respond might be to throw it back at the person offering the words. "What do you *mean*, I'll get over it? It was my sister!" Another way to respond might be with a measure of gentleness, patience, and understanding.

It's hard for people to know the right thing to say to us when we're grieving the death of someone we love. Everyone struggles to find the right words. People reach for some piece of advice or spiritual counsel or wisdom or perspective they think might help. It makes sense that when we have someone who's in pain, we want to do something. If you have a fever, you're offered a cool, wet towel for your forehead. If you break your wrist, your friends or family will take you to the hospital so you can get a cast. If you get a cut and start bleeding, someone will give you a bandage. But grief is different.

Grief requires something other than stitches or a bandage or a salve. Grief knows what it needs to help you heal: grief needs time, and it needs to be witnessed. Having a friend just sit with you and hold a space for you and be present with you can help a lot more than somebody showing up with a checklist of words they hope will "fix things" and "make it all better" and help you to "get over it."

BAILEY

Our friends have struggled to respond to well-meaning, if ill-chosen, words of advice or consolation. Bailey said, "I respond horribly when people try to tell me 'how I should feel.' No one knows exactly what you're going through, no matter how close they are to you. Grief is a hard thing to manage, so whatever you're doing for yourself is worth doing, and you should stick with it, even if other people don't understand how it's helping you."

DEXTER

Dexter also found it was important to have a sense of control over his grief process. "Some people would try to impose their opinions on me about what they thought would help me," he said. "I could see that a lot of the time, their advice was about things that would help them feel better more than it would me. My thought was, 'You know, I might as well take my own path because this is my first true experience with big grief and a big loss.' Why would I let someone else tell me how I should grieve? I wanted to make my own decisions."

JDB

In dealing with words of condolence, JDB has seen it from different angles. He said, "After my dad died, my sixth-grade teachers had the kids in my class write letters to me. They'd offer condolences or share a memory they had of my dad because he was really involved with sports. It was nice to get those letters and hear about the memories they had of my dad. . . . But I don't think the teachers checked all the letters first," he said. "There was nothing bad, but some of it was insensitive, like, 'Oh, how did he die?' But if I were in their shoes, I don't know what I'd say, either. At age eleven, all a kid knows about death is what they've seen in movies. Kids will say, 'I'm sorry for your loss,' because that's what they've heard in the movies. It's simpler and more real with my close friends. They'll just say: 'Hey, I'm here,' and that's enough."

GRACE

Grace had a similar opinion about hearing, "Sorry for your loss." Grace felt like those words were something that put distance between her and the person saying it. "Sometimes kids just don't like to hear, 'I'm sorry for your loss,'" she said. "It feels like a negative thing, not very empathetic. It's like something that people say just to end the conversation—instead of opening up to letting a kid talk." She continued, "When people find you've lost a parent, they'll start talking to you differently. You'll be talking to them, and you'll see their posture and their entire tone of voice change like they feel they have to coddle you. A lot of kids actually prefer you to keep treating them the exact same way as before. Just be normal."

Grace had good insights on another typical, but insensitive, piece of advice. "I don't like when people talk about 'just moving on,'" she said. "For kids who need to talk it out, saying, 'You should just move on' shows the kid that they shouldn't talk about it, which is not true at all. I think that my groups at Brooke's Place have really helped kids open up, kids who might have been told by somebody that 'they shouldn't talk about it,'" Grace said. "Talking is what starts the healing process. If you have a wound and just keep a Band-Aid on it, it won't heal very well. You have to take the Band-Aid off. That's what talking is—letting the wound breathe."

KATE

In Kate's experience, some of those well-meaning words came from friends who wanted to compare their own losses or their own grief to hers. "Everyone is on their journey, and you just can't compare someone else's losses to your own. I understand why it happens," Kate said. "When somebody hears about your loss, sometimes they want to compare their trauma to yours. I think it makes them feel like they're relating to you or that you have something in common. Maybe they think you'll feel better because 'their loss was greater,' and you don't have it so bad in comparison to them."

"I want to tell them to stop it. It doesn't help to have anybody's grief compared to somebody else's. That's not what life is about. Those of us who've had a loss just need to have the other person listen, to hear our story, to let us share what we've been through." Kate continued, "What we look for in life is to be loved and have our story witnessed. We need to have compassion and kindness for another person who's hurting. That's what brings people closer to each other more than anything else."

Author David Kessler might give Kate a high five for her thoughts. When Kessler talked with speaker Brené Brown on her podcast *Unlocking Us*, they discussed how people tend to compare their losses. They might want to weigh "whose loss is greater—somebody who lost a parent, or somebody whose brother died, or somebody whose best friend took their own life?" Kessler told Brown that when people get into the game of comparing loss, "I'll tell them, 'The worse loss is always your loss.'"

If a friend offers you a tone-deaf or lame condolence, you could be irritated by that—and would anybody blame you? You could, on the other hand, turn the moment into a positive both for them and for you. You could try putting into practice the virtue of forgiveness. If you can get good at strengthening this one, it'll pay you dividends far beyond your dealing with an insensitive "everything happens for a purpose."

If you're offered an unhelpful or insensitive remark of condolence, you might try telling yourself silently that "she means well, but she doesn't know the right way to say she cares." Because surely, they do care about you. You might remind yourself that they're probably doing their level best to offer some words of comfort, good advice, helpful perspective, or some kind of insight they meant to be soothing. Try telling yourself that your friend is reaching the best he can and that finding the right things to say to someone who's grieving is hard for all of us.

Try saying in your mind, silently, to the other person: "I forgive you." Here's a secret about those words: they're not for the other person, to relieve them of the responsibility for saying something hurtful; those words of forgiveness are for you, to relieve you of the burden of carrying a feeling of being hurt.

And remember that you have a choice in how you think in the first place about how to respond to insensitive words. The Stoic philosopher Marcus Aurelius wrote in his classic journal *Meditations*: "Choose not to be harmed, and you won't feel harmed. Don't feel harmed, and you haven't been." You have no control over what other people say or how they say it. But you do have control over how you think about what they said.

There's something else you can do that gives you some control and can even help strengthen the bonds of affection between you and your friend. Try to find words of your own in response, and offer them with kindness. Thank them for their words, and then take a moment to help them better understand what is most helpful to you as a grieving person. If your friend hasn't been through their grief, you probably know more about what you need than they do. It's okay to try and guide them, to speak up and let them know what you need.

Again in *Meditations*, Marcus Aurelius wrote: "People exist for one another. You can instruct or endure them." By helping to instruct and guide your friend, you show them you care enough about them to help them learn. In doing that, you can strengthen your bonds of friendship and trust. You give them a gift of empathy and understanding, which they may be able to carry forward the next time they have a friend who, like you, is dealing with the death of a loved one. Next time, they'll know better what to say. And finally, you can know for the rest of that day that, even in the midst of your grief, you were able to take something potentially hurtful and turn it into something good.

You don't even have to "correct" them either. A response can be something as simple as "Thanks for the thought. Listen, I was going to take a break and take a quiet walk through the neighborhood park. I wasn't thinking of talking all that much, but would you walk with me?"

Perhaps you might be more direct, with something like: "I appreciate your words. I'm feeling like I want to share how I'm feeling this morning. I'm not looking for advice or solace. I just feel like it would help me to have a friend like you who can just listen while I'm trying to work it out. Would you be able to help me like that?"

To go one more level up from there, you might say something like: "Thanks for the sentiments. I appreciate what you're trying to say. Do you know what kind of words I find bring some comfort? I'm not trying to tell you what to say, but just to let you know that some words seem to help more than others. Things like: 'Go ahead and say what's in your heart; I'm not going anywhere' or 'I'm with you, okay? You're not alone. Do you want to sit for a while?' Or just, 'I'm here. You talk. I'll listen.' Those kinds of words really help me. Okay? I appreciate your friendship so much."

It may feel like you shouldn't have to be doing all the heavy lifting to get what you need in a time of grief, right? You're the one who had your sister or your mother die. Shouldn't other people—your friends and family—be helping you? Fair point.

In trying to answer that question, it's useful to take the perspective that we're all learning here. Life? It's something we're all doing for the first time (as far as we know). Every joy and every pain that someone else experiences, we'll experience too. Everything that we endure, other people will endure those things also. The best thing we can do is to be kind to one another along the journey.

In his book *The End of Faith*, philosopher and podcast host Sam Harris writes: "Every person you have ever met, every person you will pass in the street today, is going to die. Living long enough, each will suffer the loss of his friends and family. All are going to lose everything they love in this world. Why would one want to be anything but kind to them in the meantime?"

WORKING THROUGH FAMILY STUFF

When a family member dies, all the other family relationships can get especially hard. If a sister dies, not only have you lost a sister, but your parents have lost a daughter, and your grandmother has lost a granddaughter. If you have other brothers and sisters, they each had their unique relationship with their sister. Everyone has their ways of grieving, and one brother's way of dealing with a sister's loss may be different from how you might grieve.

Plus, when something as huge as the death of a family member happens, the relationships between everybody else in the family can change too. Sometimes relationships can get scrambled. Your mom might need support as if she were the kid and you were the adult. Your younger siblings might look to you to be a stand-in for a parent who's died, or maybe for a parent who's physically there but not fully present.

BAILEY

Bailey has worked with a lot of these family challenges. "After my sister died, I felt that both my mom and my dad needed my support. Looking back, I wish that they were the ones giving me the support I needed. I just always felt like I had to stay strong for them, which I think is one reason why I pushed my feelings about Sydney inside," Bailey said.

KATE

Family relationships can be complicated even before a family member dies and can get more complicated afterward. Kate's mom struggled with addiction issues, and because of that, Kate, as the oldest of four kids, felt like she had been stuck in a caregiver role. "Because of my mom's addictions, I spent a lot of time taking care of my younger siblings even before my mom died. My little sister said once, 'You know, you're kind of like our pseudo-mom. But I also want you as a sister.' I would tell her, 'I am your sister, but if I see that you need help, I want to help.' I did have to be stern with them when I was younger. But I was only thirteen years old, and what does a thirteen-year-old know about the world? Not a lot." Kate continued, "For kids who've had a parent die related to substance abuse, it's important to realize that your 'normal wasn't

---

normal' even before that person died. You were stuck in a dysfunctional dynamic. When that person dies, sometimes you can recover stability and have a chance at a normal life that wasn't possible before. You're not stuck in that cycle of abuse. After my mom died, the counseling helped me gain some self-awareness of how my role needed to change, and how I could be a sister again instead of a pseudo-mom. You can take that toxic dynamic that used to be 'your normal' and change it into something beautiful—a normal where you have people there who love you and care for you."

JDB

In JDB's life, he was old enough to recognize tension in his parents' relationship even before his dad's death. "My parents got divorced the year before my dad died," JDB said. "I was only in sixth grade, and I don't think they realized I knew what was going on, but I did. After he died, family stuff was awkward. It felt weird to be around my mom's side of the family, knowing that there was tension about my dad over their divorce. It was hard with Mom for a while, but we've been able to patch everything up. It would have helped me if I could have had a better understanding earlier about why the family was upset with my dad." Despite these bouts of tension, his family was also a source of strength for JDB. He said, "We spent a lot of time with extended family when I was a kid growing up. A lot of them were age thirty and up, so I think that spending time with family who were triple my age helped me mature faster. I think that helped me deal with things when my dad died."

BAILEY

Family relationships can get more complicated when everyone is trying to deal with their grief in their own ways. Bailey said, "My mom became much more needy after my sister died. She wanted to spend a lot of time with me and always wanted to make sure that I was okay. At the time, I didn't like it, but looking back on it, I appreciate that I wasn't alone." Bailey's relationship with her dad came under a different kind of pressure. "I feel like Dad pulled away from me. I feel like we stopped talking as much and avoided anything related to Sydney. I don't feel as close to him anymore like I used to when Sydney was alive," she said. Larger family gatherings can sometimes be a source of unease for Bailey too. "I'm always afraid of family get-togethers because I know Sydney will come up in some way, shape, or form," she said. "I'm afraid to feel my grief publicly in front of them. I'm afraid of how my family members and others will react to my grief and the feelings I may have towards what's brought up. I'm not sure what I'd say to other teens, as I'm still struggling to figure out how to confront the fear I have." Is it reassuring to know that other kids who've been down the same road don't have it all figured out yet and that you don't have to have it all figured out either?

DEXTER

For others of our friends, their relationships with their parents changed in other ways. When Dexter arrived home from school that day and was the one to find his dad, he said to himself, "'Well, here we go. Now I gotta be strong.' I called the police, and I was the one to tell my mom. That was the hardest part. I knew I was taking a big step and that I was going to have to be strong for myself— and for Mom," Dexter said. "My dad always told me that I needed to be strong for whatever might come. I just decided this was my time to be strong for my mom. But God, it's been hard since." In some ways, that experience has helped Dexter's relationship with his mother. "I felt like I needed to spend a lot of time with my mom during the first weeks after my dad died because it was just so fresh, and I felt like I wanted the security of being near her," Dexter said. "With us supporting each other, it was a balance. And we're still trying to figure it out today. We try to make sure that we're each hearing each other because we do need communication. And that's what we thrive on. I'm lucky to have her."

JDB

JDB's appreciation for his mother increased after his dad died. He said, "I would think about how you never know what can happen to the other people in your life, and feeling afraid that something else might happen. I'm glad that my mom is really healthy, and that makes me feel more confident about her being around, which is nice."

LOGAN

Logan has felt a sense of protectiveness for his younger brother from the start. "There are four years' age difference between him and me," Logan said. "I remember going into the hospital room when he was born, seeing him in that little plastic tub. I looked at him and thought, 'Man, this older-brother thing is going to be great.'" Logan's sense of responsibility for his brother increased after their father died. "I feel like it's part of my job to take care of him now and make sure he remembers our dad and what kind of person he was. Me and my brother have a lot of the same hobbies. We love to fish and target shoot together," he said.

GRACE

As one of three siblings, Grace's experience with grieving her father was different than her older sister's (who has stronger memories of their dad) and different from her younger brother's (who has fewer memories than Grace has). She said, "My grief experience was different from my older sister's and my younger brother's. I was four when our dad died, and my sister was nine. So she grew up with my father for almost ten years. For her, it wasn't just 'not having someone.' It was 'having someone and then losing them,'" Grace said. "My sister has more memories of our dad, so it probably hurt more for her. She got to be with him and then lost him. I didn't get the first part—I just lost him. Then for my little brother, he's a little more emotional," Grace said. "Sometimes he'll walk into my room, and I'm like, 'What's wrong?' and he'll say, 'I miss Daddy.' I'll say, 'I'm sorry,' and I'll try to comfort him as much as I can. With the three of us together, my sister can call up a memory of our dad. We can share that memory, and we can comfort each other. I think it brings us closer together."

PART III

CARRYING ON

We started this journey together by talking about how you are not alone. Other people—teens and adults—have experienced grief and loss before you, and they have gifts of insight and support that are free for the taking. On your road ahead, you'll surely meet others who find themselves also in the grip of sadness, loss, and grief—and you may find that part of your healing may be found in sharing what you've learned, as those before you have shared with you. When we say, "You are not alone," it might be truer to say, "None of us are alone." That's a universal truth that will always endure.

How do you carry on? The answer might simply be, "The best you can." You will not "move on." How could you? A best friend, a brother or sister, a mother or father who has died—they will always be with you. There is no "moving on" from their memory and the love you have for them. But it is possible to move forward. It is possible to live fully, with meaning and purpose, and carrying the love you feel for your person and go forward with a life that honors them and you.

No recipes exist for living fully. No checklists. No pass-fail tests. In the conversations our friends have shared with us throughout these pages, it's easy to see that no one thing works for everybody. Grief support groups work for some teens, and others find more help in one-on-one counseling. Some kids find release and insight by writing in a journal, and some do not.

Most have moments of peace and acceptance, which might be followed shortly by an unexpected grief-storm of longing. There's no "happy ending" to the loss of someone you love. But there can be a sense of contentment in the feeling of making progress toward wholeness and living a fulfilling life on the road ahead.

CHAPTER FOURTEEN

SAYING THEIR NAME AND KEEPING THEM CLOSE

I n the National Geographic documentary "*The Story of God with Morgan Freeman*," the episode titled "Beyond Death" contains a conversation between Freeman and Egyptologist Salima Ikram. Ikram explains why the names of pharaohs were carved so deeply into the stones of their burial chambers. She says, "The name is one of the most important things. If you have your name written down and people say it, your spirit is given this burst of energy." She continues, "The Temple of Millions of Years was built by Rameses III to give him eternal life. You carve the name deeply so it will not be erased, it will be remembered, and you will live forever."

Three thousand years after Rameses III, British science fiction writer Terry Pratchett said the same thing in his novel *Going Postal*: "Haven't you ever heard the saying 'A man's not dead while his name is still spoken'?" Whether or not you believe the ancient Egyptians or Terry Pratchett, there's still good reason to say your person's name (even if you're not quite sure about their spirit being infused with energy). It might be easier to think that a part of your person does live in you. When you say their name, whatever part of them that is alive in you is sharing in the energy of your thoughts and your love. And maybe that's enough.

On top of saying their name, carrying mementos of your person can also help keep their memory alive for you. In his 2019 memoir *Dad's Maybe Book*, novelist Tim O'Brien (you may have read his classic *The Things They Carried*) reflects on his father's ashes that he keeps nearby:

A few feet from me, my dad's urn—his own bronze stewpot—sits on a wide mahogany shelf filled with books, sixty or seventy of them, a resting place that is fitting for a man who so dearly loved to read. Perhaps like other sons, I sometimes talk to the ashes in the urn. I ask for advice. I tell secrets. I express my love. Although nothing ever comes back to me, I've grown accustomed to the silence and do not really mind because my dad is here in this room, on a shelf, just a few feet away, and I know he wants to speak but simply cannot.

DEXTER

Many of our friends follow Tim O'Brien's lead in different ways. Dexter and his mom brought his father's ashes home. "We still have my dad's urn in the house," Dexter said. "Mom wanted to put the urn in a corner. I said we should put it where everybody can see him. She didn't want to feel weird about it, but I said, 'You know, he's an important person. Why don't we do that?'"

"I know he's gone from this physical realm, but I sometimes feel like I can still communicate with him," Dexter said. "To the thin air, sometimes I'll say, 'Hey, how you doing, Dad?' Then I'll wait a few seconds and pay attention. Sometimes I'll feel like I get something back. It might be as small a feeling as a wrinkle changing on my shirt. I can feel like he's listening and hearing me. Then these good memories of my dad will just start pouring into my head. Even though I didn't ask for them, I really appreciate them. When that happens, I make sure to say thank you."

LOGAN

Special places that represent a connection between our person and us can be a way to stay connected with them. Logan said, "Me and my dad went to car shows a lot when I was growing up, and we worked on project cars together. I inherited his '72 Chevy pickup. When I want to see my dad or talk to him or have some good memories, I'll go down and sit in the pickup and just talk to him. I feel like he's there."

JDB

JDB talked about mementos that help him feel like he's keeping his father close. He held up his wrist and proudly showed a pair of bracelets. "These are actually my dad's," he said. "When I was ten, I braided this paracord bracelet myself and gave it to him. He wore it every day until the day he died. That's why I never take it off. Like ever."

He pointed to the other bracelet and said, "My dad used to wear this leather one, too." He tugged at the leather bracelet, and it seemed like he was picturing it on his dad's wrist. "You can see how it's stretched," JDB said. "He had bigger wrists than me."

DEXTER

Dexter also wore something that belonged to his father. "One thing of my dad's that I keep with me, weirdly enough, are his shoelaces. I took them out of his shoes, and I've got them laced into my own shoes," Dexter said. "It makes me feel a little bit better knowing I've got a part of him with me. Now, whenever I'm walking, it's like we're always walking together." Dexter lit up when he said, "Plus, who else is gonna do something like that?"

JDB

Sometimes we can memorialize our person and keep them close through the choices we make for our own lives going forward. JDB felt like he was staying close by deciding to follow in his dad's career footsteps. "When I graduate high school in a couple of years, I'm thinking of studying business in college," he said. "All my dad's buddies say he had an aptitude for business, and I think I inherited some of his skills, academic-wise. I got a 104 in my high school

After his father died, Dexter took the laces from his father's boots and laced them into his own, so he could always be walking with his father. *Illustration by Kate Haberer*

business class, so I plan on trying for a scholarship at a college with a good business school."

BAILEY

Bailey has a few ways she tries to honor her sister Sydney and keep her close. "I'll go back and look through Sydney's social media pictures and find the ones of our times together. I celebrate her birthdays. At Christmas, we hang Sydney's stocking and her Christmas tree ornaments. When my sister Beth got married, we set a place for Sydney at the bridal party table," she said.

Bailey was proud of starting two STEM clubs for girls at local elementary schools to help foster their interest in science and technology. "I was able to get the clubs named 'SMB'—Sydney's initials," she said, "so those clubs are dedicated in honor of her."

GRACE

Grace keeps it pretty simple with the mementos. "I've kept a picture in my locker for three years now. It's a picture of my dad and my entire family. I'm in it, and I'm probably three or something," Grace said. "It's a pretty old photo, but that's one thing I like to keep close."

There are different ways you can carry your person's spirit and memory forward with you. You might run a 5K or 10K wearing a T-shirt bearing their name or picture. In the 2010 movie *The Way*, the character played by Martin Sheen backpacks the five-hundred-mile Camino de Santiago pilgrim trail in northern Spain and carries his son's ashes along the way. If Spain is too far to travel, the U.S. has many millions of acres of public land, and epic routes available like the Appalachian Trail or the Pacific Crest Trail, where you might take a long hike in their memory.

You might help keep your person's memory alive by volunteering to serve causes that were important to them. Nonprofits that advocate for clean water and air, social justice, or child welfare are always looking for volunteers who have a sense of purpose. Groups that help people with addictions, focus on suicide prevention, or provide grief support would be glad to have a young volunteer whose life has been touched by challenges like these. It would make it easy to answer a question like, "Why are you volunteering on a suicide prevention hotline?" The answer could be as simple as, "I'm doing it for my sister."

Honoring the life of your person who died can be as simple as wearing their wristwatch, lacing up their boots on your feet, saying their name out loud, or serving causes that honor them. These small rituals can help you feel like you're keeping them close by and that you're keeping a space where their memory can live with you as you move forward in your life. Who knows . . . when you say their name, perhaps it's not too much to believe that they might just hear your voice.

CHAPTER FIFTEEN

FINDING MEANING

Millions of people have watched the documentaries by filmmaker Ken Burns. Burns talks about why he thinks people have flocked to watch his films about the Civil War, baseball, Lewis and Clark, the national parks, and country music. Burns says that in this world of six-second videos and 140-character text messages, we're starved for meaning.

This need for meaning may be what leads people to offer those clumsy (even if well-meaning) pep talks with words like, "Everything happens for a reason." They're bouncing around the edges of "meaning" but just don't know the right words.

David Kessler is an author and grief expert who himself struggled to find meaning after the sudden death of his twenty-one-year-old son. In his 2019 book *Finding Meaning: The Sixth Stage of Grief,* Kessler writes that "meaning comes through finding a way to sustain your love for the person after their death, while you're moving forward with your life."

KATE

Kate has an understanding of what it meant to find meaning going forward after her mother died. She flipped through pictures on her phone. In every photo, she was in an embrace with her friends: groups of kids with their arms around each other, leaning toward the camera, a friend on her lap, or she on theirs. Kate said, "I think that loss is something that happens to you. You can't control what happens, but you can find the meaning in how you take that loss and cultivate it into something that helps you grow. How you deal

---

with loss is part of how you find out who you are as a person. . . .
I want to find my meaning in how I help other people," Kate said.
"Because of how things were when I was growing up, I've had to
persevere and never give up. If I can use what I've learned to help
others, I feel like that will be meaningful. I want to take what I've
learned and help people by becoming a doctor. Some people go to
medical school for the money or the title. I don't care about any of
that. I want my profession to be one where I can serve, where I can
bring something beautiful to people's lives and to build this web of
connections. Kids are hurting like I was. I want to show them that
there's someone there for them, someone to help them deal with
their pain and loss. I feel like I'm paying it forward."

GRACE

Grace finds meaning by staying involved in her grief support group
for young people at Brooke's Place in central Indiana. As Kate does,
Grace also finds a sense of meaning in sharing what she's learned
with other kids who are earlier on in their grief process. "When
you're a kid, it's hard to have a grasp on the concept of death. As
I get older and as other people in my life die, I find that it doesn't
hurt less . . . it always hurts. But I find it easier to heal that hurt
because I understand the process better. Kids get told that 'it gets
better,' but they don't always believe it. I want to tell them that it
really does get better."

BAILEY

Bailey had talked about finding meaning after her sister's death by
starting STEM programs for girls in local elementary schools and
naming the groups in her sister's honor. Other kids have found
meaning by pursuing a career that their parent followed, or maybe
going into cancer medicine after their best friend died of leukemia.
On the other hand, a life of meaning might not have anything to
do with careers or projects, but might simply be living a life of
resilience and strength and being of service to other people.

When Bailey's sister Sydney died, her grief made Bailey's other family relationships difficult. Bailey memorialized her sister by creating a STEM club in Sydney's honor. *Illustration by Kate Haberer*

Author Jordan Peterson has talked about seeking a life of meaning rather than a life of happiness. If our main goal is happiness, and then the storms of life roll through—which they always will—we will be left with nothing as "happiness" blows away in the storm. Happiness is good, and we can cherish it and appreciate it when it appears; it will always be part of our life experiences. But if we first pursue meaning and purpose, those things can be sustained even amid the storms. Peterson says, "The purpose of life, as far as I can tell, is to find a mode of being that's so meaningful that the fact that 'life is suffering' is no longer relevant."

This resilience is something that Austrian psychiatrist and Holocaust survivor Viktor Frankl wrote about in his classic 1946 book *Man's Search for Meaning*. Of his fellow prisoners in the Nazi concentration camps, Frankl observed that

> the prisoners who seemed to have the best chance of survival were not necessarily the strongest or physically healthiest, but those somehow capable of directing their thoughts towards a sense of meaning. A few prisoners were "able to retreat from their terrible surroundings to a life of inner riches and spiritual freedom," and in the imagining of such a space, there was the potential for survival.

If a person can survive the Holocaust and find a way to live fully, does that mean it is possible for us to live through pain and great loss too? One of Frankl's most often-quoted insights from this book is: "What is to give light must endure burning."

There's one more level of "living with meaning" to consider. There's a question that people ask about meaning. It's sometimes even asked as a joke because it seems so unanswerable: "What is the meaning of life?"

There's an excellent documentary you can find on YouTube, called *HUMAN: The Movie*. The filmmakers spent three years collecting interviews from two thousand men, women, and kids from sixty different countries. Each of them speaks in their own language about love and loss, deprivation and plenty, anger and forgiveness, and their hopes for better lives for themselves and their kids.

In one of the final interviews, a Brazilian man named Argus responds to the filmmaker's question "What do you think is the meaning of life?" Argus thinks for a moment and chuckles as he asks if the filmmaker can ask him an easier question. He has clear hazel eyes and a close-cropped beard, and he answers in his native Portuguese:

> The meaning of life? Sometimes I think of a phrase I heard as a boy, a friend who said: "Life is like carrying a message from the child you were, to the old man you will be. You have to make sure that this message isn't lost along the way." I often think of that, because when I was little, I used to imagine fine things, to dream of a world without beggars in which everyone was happy. Simple, subtle things. But you lose those things over the course of life. You just work to be able to buy things. And you stop seeing the beggar. You stop caring. You think, where is the message of the child I once was? Maybe the meaning of life is making sure that this message doesn't disappear.

Maybe "finding meaning" throughout this process of grieving is just that: to carry that love for your person forward, not letting the flame go out. Making sure that when you get to be the old man or old woman you will eventually become, you are tending the flame of your love for your mother, your father, your brother, your sister, or your good friend.

CHAPTER SIXTEEN
REWRITING YOUR RELATIONSHIP

After your person dies and the first wave of numbness starts to recede, you might have the thought: "This is not the future as I thought it would be." Your relationship with your sister was supposed to be a story that included: "We'll each grow up to have children, and we'll be aunts to each other's kids, and we'll be at all their birthday parties." The story with your father was supposed to have a chapter about sharing a beer on your twenty-first birthday and driving to Montana to go fly-fishing for a week. Your best friend wasn't supposed to overdose. You were supposed to be roommates when you went to college.

Those relationships aren't possible anymore, even though you long dearly for them. You can't just put that relationship on the shelf and leave it behind, either. If neither of those choices is possible, and if it's true that we write the stories of our lives, maybe it's possible to rewrite our relationship with our person who's died. Is there a way to write that story in a way that you can carry your person forward with you? Love doesn't die, so maybe the relationship can live on, but in another form. While it may not be the relationship as you thought it would be, it might be a relationship that can honor them and can also enrich you.

Author Elizabeth Gilbert (who wrote *Eat Pray Love*) was able to embrace the grief of knowing that the future she pictured with her partner Rayya was no longer possible after Rayya's death. In a conversation on Marie Forleo's website, Gilbert said, "The puzzle I'm sitting with is this: there was a life that I could only have with Rayya. And that life is no longer available. And there is a life that I can only have without Rayya, and that life is just beginning. There's a whole changed world without her, and I'm equally fascinated by what that one is." Gilbert continued, "I think the real sense of creative adventure is for me to say yes ahead of time to the new one because I don't know what it is yet. But I'm in. Show me."

As you wrap your arms and your mind around knowing that your mother or father or sibling or your best friend will no longer be part of this journey in the way you'd pictured it, you can reimagine the story as part of a creative journey into the unknown, as Gilbert did. While the death of your person is "something that happened to you" and is something over which you have no control, the creative part is in what you do have control over, how you choose to think about your loss.

The longer we live, the more we have a chance to recognize that pain is inevitable: it's evidence that we have loved. "Suffering," on the other hand, is optional and something over which we have a choice. Is it possible to rewrite your relationship with your person in a way that lets you take control and define a new role for yourself, on your own terms? Can your story acknowledge your pain without stoking the suffering?

LOGAN

Take, for example, Logan's relationship with his dad, Marcus. Logan will always be Marcus's son, but that father-son relationship is different now that Marcus had died. Part of how Logan has been able to rewrite his relationship with his dad is to recognize that while they won't be working on project cars together, part of Marcus is present in that '72 Chevy pickup that Logan inherited. Their relationship now lives differently: in Logan's memories and how he imagines his dad exists now. "What I hope for, how I try to picture him, is that wherever my dad is, he's got a nice cigar in his mouth, on a beach with a beer in one hand and a fishing rod in the other hand," Logan said. "What else do I hope for? I hope to realize that wherever he is, no matter what you believe in or whether you're religious and believe in heaven, or believe in reincarnation or whatever; I just want to picture that he's in his perfect spot. I

Logan and his father would fix cars together. When his dad died, Logan was angry at him for leaving. He found that group therapy helped him talk about his experiences. Eventually, the pickup truck they used to work on became a place Logan could feel close to his father. *Illustration by Kate Haberer*

think of Dad on a Harley with a lady on the backseat. I see him in the woods and enjoying his life." In a way, Logan has been able to rewrite his story, to redefine his relationship with his dad and be able to hold in his imagination that his father is present in a perfect spot. This vision gives him a sense of fulfillment in feeling like his dad is okay.

The story of our relationship with our person can feature us as the one who carries their memory forward. We keep part of them alive by saying their names, wearing their laces in our boots, telling our stories about them, and being a living legacy to the truth that they were here on this earth, for however long.

BAILEY

Bailey has done her best to try and adjust or rewrite her idea of what "normal" means, and to establish some way to relate to her sister's memory. "Before Sydney died, that was when life felt 'normal.' She was involved in every aspect of my life in some way," Bailey said. "I feel like now everything is different, and it's not going back to that normal feeling that I had before. So now I guess my 'normal' feeling is 'feeling unnormal,' if that makes any sense. I think now I'm having more good days than bad, but I don't think the grief and pain will ever truly go away. It will always be a part of me. In the end, I believe it's still possible to be happy and have a peaceful life, even without your person in it. It's just that you have to find a different kind of happiness than the kind you had when they were still alive."

JDB

JDB has been able to recast his relationship with his dad by recognizing the parallels in their lives. "My dad lost his own dad when he was about my age," JDB said. "His dad was his best friend, too, just like my dad and me were best friends. Then my dad lost his brother in a drunk driving accident, and his brother was also my dad's best friend. I could see how my dad lived through a lot of sadness that

I didn't comprehend at first. . . . But I was able to see that his life wasn't just about him being sad and lonely," JDB continued. "I want to learn that from him. He was always bringing people close, even though he'd experienced a lot of loss in his own life. I could see that even with all my dad had lived through, having a father and a brother die, he could still be happy. That helped me see that I can be happy, too."

GRACE

Because Grace's father died when she was so young, she's had more time than many of our other friends to redefine her relationship with her dad. She's able to relate to him and his memory in a way that she can handle, and most days are pretty good. "I'm pretty far down the road," she said. "When my dad comes to mind, the lows are less low than they used to be. If I started focusing on it, I can get upset—but I won't be as upset as maybe five years ago."

In his books about grief, David Kessler writes about the legacy: that part of our person that we carry forward in our own lives. He asks whether we think our person would want their legacy to be that the sadness of their loss destroyed us. Or would they want their legacy to be that we went forward with a life of exploration and adventure and love—a life that honors them and their memory? Perhaps our gift to them is that we give them that fertile place where their memory and spirit can continue to exist.

In rewriting our relationship with our person who died, and giving ourselves the broader perspective of carrying their life forward, we might find some meaning in a passage from *The Prophet* by Khalil Gibran:

When you part from your friend, you grieve not; For that which you love most in him may be clearer in his absence, as the mountain to the climber is clearer from the plain.

CHAPTER SEVENTEEN

NEW CHAPTERS AHEAD

Your life is your story. Part of your story is written for you, at least in the beginning. You're born on this continent or that one, to these parents or those. Your story comes with the language you learned to speak as a child. Your story gives you a gender, and it gives you the color of your eyes.

After those first chapters, though, you eventually turn to a next page, to a new chapter, and you find that the page is blank. You are free to write the next paragraphs and pages and chapters of your life. You are also free to rewrite the story if that story is no longer serving you well.

You get to make choices of what characters to include, what the plot will be, and what happens to the hero—and that hero is you. You're on your own hero's journey. You can write it, rewrite it, and rewrite it again, as you wish. Unexpected plot twists may arise, but you're the author.

The poet Mary Oliver recognized that we have the power to decide how to write those chapters of our short lives. Her poem "The Summer Day" concludes:

> Tell me, what else should I have done?
> Doesn't everything die at last, and too soon?
> Tell me, what is it you plan to do
> With your one wild and precious life?

171

KATE

Kate is a fan of Mary Oliver's poetry. In reflecting on how she thinks about rewriting the plan for her own wild and precious journey, Kate said, "In life, there are all these little chapters where you're learning something about yourself. You're born, you're a child, and then you go through all the chapters to adulthood. Each of those chapters has lessons about recognizing that there will be tribulations and trials. And you figure out how to move through those trials. Losing someone is going to happen to all of us eventually. When you do lose someone, you might never get over it fully. You probably never will," Kate said. "But you can find a middle place in the story where the feeling of loss is manageable, a place where you can live your life," she said. "The grief will still be there, but you can move forward and set your goals and turn your dreams into something real. I can look at my own loss as something that's pushed me to where I am now, to be who I am now."

DEXTER

Dexter talked about his life's journey as something of a book. He said, "The year my dad died was one of the heaviest chapters in my life. It was a dark tale, but it's gotten lighter and brighter with each volume. I'm not totally there yet, but I'm getting closer. The chapters aren't as dark. They're brighter"—he paused and chuckled—"maybe more of an off-brand white. I feel happy with the way the chapters have progressed, and I'm able to see positive changes as I've worked through my grief."

It's no secret that documentary filmmaker Ken Burns knows something about telling stories. He was given his first movie camera and made his first film when he was seventeen. Millions of people have watched his documentaries about baseball and Jackie Robinson, or Susan B. Anthony and women's voting rights, or the Civil War and Abraham Lincoln, or jazz, or country music.

Burns also knows something about grief. In a short YouTube video called "Ken Burns: On Story," he talks about what it was like for him to know that his mother had cancer from the time he was a little kid, and how she died when he was eleven. Burns says:

> It might be that what I'm engaged in, in a historical pursuit, is a thinly or perhaps thickly disguised waking of the dead, that I try to make Abraham Lincoln and Jackie Robinson and Louis Armstrong come alive. It may be very obvious and very close to home who I'm actually trying to wake up. . . . We have to keep the wolf from the door, you know? We tell stories to continue ourselves. We all think an exception is going to be made in our case and that we're going to live forever. "Being a human" is actually arriving at the understanding that that's not going to be. "Story" is there to just remind us that it's just okay.

We can find comfort in hearing the stories of others who have also suffered a loss. We find the healing power of an empathetic listener who will sit and witness our grief as we tell our own stories about our person who died, what they mean to us, and how we miss them. You're not alone. We can embrace the freedom that comes from the knowledge that we can rewrite the very story we're in and change the plot going forward. We can use the stories of our lives to keep the flame alive for our person who died and give them a place to live within us.

Novelist Cormac McCarthy has thought about this idea of "keeping the flame going." In his 2006 novel *The Road* (which earned a Pulitzer Prize for Fiction and was later made into a movie you may have seen), there's a recurring line about fire. In this story, the world is dying. It's cold, and nothing is growing. We don't know what happened exactly. All Cormac tells us: "The clocks stopped at 1:17. A long shear of light and then a series of low concussions."

The main characters are a father and his young son. The father himself is slowly dying, but he's trying to protect his son and trying to get him somewhere safe. They're "on the road," heading south toward the coast, hoping to find people, food, warmth, security.

Throughout the novel, the father repeats three times to his son that the boy is "carrying the fire." Nothing bad will happen to us, we won't do wrong ourselves, and you will recognize the good people when you find them—because they also are "carrying the fire." In the end, as the father lies dying, the boy pleads to go with him. The father says, "You can't. You have to carry the fire." His father dies, and the boy stays with him for three days.

After those three days, the boy, now an orphan and alone, ventures back onto the road. He soon encounters "a veteran" and his family: a wife and two children, the first the boy has seen throughout the entire novel. Remembering his father's words about how to identify the "good guys," he asks the veteran, "Are you carrying the fire?" The veteran has no idea what the boy is talking about, but it seems to him the right answer is "Yes." The veteran's wife puts her arms around the boy and holds him.

You carry the fire. You carry it for your mother who died. You carry it for your father who passed away. You carry it for your brother or sister or good friend who is no longer here with you.

You carry the fire for yourself as you are now, and you carry it for the older you who is down the road and waiting for you. Your older self needs the fire you are carrying. That fire is the story of your life and the story of the people you love, whether they are living or dead. It's a story you get to write from here forward.

Now carry your fire. Go live your story.

RESOURCES

SUPPORT GROUPS AND RESOURCES

Brooke's Place (Indianapolis, IN): brookesplace.org

The Dougy Center (Portland, OR): dougy.org

Grief Healing Discussion Groups: griefhealingdiscussiongroups
.com

Grieving.com Forums: forums.grieving.com

WinterSpring (Medford, OR): winterspring.org

WEBSITES

AfterTalk: www.aftertalk.com/grief_organizations

American Cancer Society—Seeking Help and Support for Grief
and Loss: cancer.org/treatment/end-of-life-care/grief-and-loss/
depression-and-complicated-grief

Grief.com: Because Love Never Dies: grief.com

The Grief Dialogues: griefdialogues.com/share-your-story

Hello Grief: hellogrief.org

Kara: kara-grief.org/support-for/teens-and-children

Modern Loss: modernloss.com

National Alliance for Grieving Children: childrengrieve.org

The National Foundation for Grieving Children, Teens and Families: alittlehope.org

Open to Hope: opentohope.com

What's Your Grief? whatsyourgrief.com

MEDITATION APPS AND RESOURCES

Breathe2Relax—relaxation app

Calm—meditation app

Headspace—meditation app

10% Happier—meditation app

Waking Up—meditation app

Meditation: A simple, fast way to reduce stress (Mayo Clinic): mayoclinic.org/tests-procedures/meditation/in-depth/meditation/art-20045858

Mindful magazine: mindful.org

7 Ways Meditation Can Actually Change the Brain: forbes.com/sites/alicegwalton/2015/02/09/7-ways-meditation-can-actually-change-the-brain

Tara Brach: tarabrach.com

A Two-Minute Guide to How to Meditate (Dan Harris): brainpickings.org/2016/09/16/how-to-meditate-animation

HOTLINES

GriefShare: 1-800-395-5755

Teen Health & Wellness: teenhealthandwellness.com/static/hotlines—Grief and Loss

BOOKS

Extremely Loud and Incredibly Close, by Jonathan Safran Foer

The Fault in Our Stars, by John Green

History Is All You Left Me, by Adam Silvera

Mindfulness and Grief, by Heather Stang

Motherless Daughters, by Hope Edelman

Never the Same: Coming to Terms with the Death of a Parent, by Donna Schuurman

On Children and Death: How Children and Their Parents Can and Do Cope with Death, by Elisabeth Kübler-Ross
On Grieving the Death of a Father, by Harold Ivan Smith
Things I Wish I Knew before My Mom Died: Coping with Loss Every Day, by Ty Alexander

POETRY

"Hope Is the Thing with Feathers," by Emily Dickinson
"One Art," by Elizabeth Bishop
"A Parable of Immortality," by Luther F. Beecher

MUSIC

"Adagio for Strings," by Samuel Barber
"Angel Flying Too Close to the Ground," by Willie Nelson
"Colder Weather," by the Zac Brown Band
"Come Wake Me Up," by Rascal Flatts
"If We Were Vampires," by Jason Isbell
"Supermarket Flowers," by Ed Sheeran
"Tears in Heaven," by Eric Clapton
"Timshel," by Mumford & Sons

PODCASTS AND PODCAST EPISODES

Karen Armstrong: "Steps to a Compassionate Life," on *Super Soul Conversations* with Oprah Winfrey, https://youtu.be/wCDrBm RsmAc
Checking in with Susan David: Moving Forward with Grief: https://podcasts.apple.com/us/podcast/checking-in-with-susan-david/id1504596643
Grief, Love, Heal (iTunes)
Grief Out Loud: The Dougy Center (iTunes)

David Kessler: "Grief and Finding Meaning," on *Unlocking Us* with Brené Brown, https://brenebrown.com/podcast/david-kessler-and-brene-on-grief-and-finding-meaning/

B. J. Miller: "The Man Who Studied 1,000 Deaths to Learn How to Live," on *The Tim Ferriss Show*, https://tim.blog/2016/04/14/bj-miller/

Mindfulness & Grief (iTunes)

Open to Hope (iTunes)

Elaine Pagels: "How Hearts Can Heal after Tragedy," on *Fresh Air* with Terry Gross, npr.org/2018/11/05/664347954/why-religion-asks-how-hearts-can-heal-after-tragedy

SoundCloud—StoryCorps, https://soundcloud.com/user-51900 4320

Terrible, Thanks for Asking: Nora McInerny (iTunes)

What's Your Grief (iTunes)

Terry Tempest Williams: "Finding Beauty in a Broken World," on *Insights at the Edge* with Tami Simon podcast

MOVIES AND TELEVISION SHOWS

City of Angels
The Descendants
Extremely Loud & Incredibly Close
Ghost
Hachi: A Dog's Tale
Manchester by the Sea
Taking Chance
This Is Us
The Way
What Dreams May Come

VIDEOS

Kasim Al-Mashat: "How Mindfulness Meditation Redefines Pain," youtu.be/JVwLjC5etEQ

The Dougy Center: youtube.com/user/DougyCenter1

Tim Ferriss and Zen Hospice Project Dr. B. J. Miller: https://tim .blog/2016/04/14/bj-miller/

Elizabeth Gilbert, on grief while writing *City of Girls*: marieforleo .com/2019/06/elizabeth-gilbert-city-of-girls/

Lori Gottlieb: "How Changing Your Story Can Change Your Life," youtu.be/O_MQr4lHm0c

Hank Green: "The Sudden Obliteration of Expectation," https:// youtu.be/cCNW9jO7EyM

Sam Harris: "A Lesson on Gratitude," https://youtu .be/2CbI0WOcUGo

How to meditate in two minutes: brainpickings.org/2016/09/16/ how-to-meditate-animation

Anne Lamott: "12 Truths I Learned from Life and Writing," ted .com/talks/anne_lamott_12_truths_i_learned_from_life_and_ writing

Nora McInerny: "We Don't Move On from Grief, We Move Forward with It," ted.com/talks/nora_mcinerny_we_don_t_ move_on_from_grief_we_move_forward_with_it?

Alyssa Monks: "How Loss Helped One Artist Find Beauty in Imperfection," ted.com/talks/alyssa_monks_how_loss_helped_ one_artist_find_beauty_in_imperfection

Jason Rosenthal: "The Journey through Loss and Grief," ted.com/ talks/jason_b_rosenthal_the_journey_through_loss_and_ grief?language=en

Three-minute mindful breathing exercise: youtu.be/SEfs5TJZ6Nk

Yoga with Adriene: https://www.youtube.com/user/yogawithadriene

DOCUMENTARIES

Speaking Grief: speakinggrief.org
The Story of God with Morgan Freeman, Season 1, Episode 6,
   "Beyond Death." National Geographic Channel, 2016
Voices of Grief: voicesofgrief.org

SOCIAL MEDIA

Academy of Grief: @AcademyofGrief
AfterTalk: @grievingandloss
The Dougy Center: @thedougycenter
GriefHelp: @GriefHelp
The Grief Toolbox: @TheGriefToolbox
HealGrief.org: @HealGrief
David Kessler: @IamDavidKessler
Modern Loss: @ModernLoss
Navigating Grief: @NavigateGrief
WhatsYourGrief: @WhatsYourGrief

BIBLIOGRAPHY

al-Khater, Abdullah. *Grief & Depression from an Islamic Perspective.* London: Al-Firdous, 2001.

Augenthaler, Debbie. *You Are Not Alone: A Heartfelt Guide for Grief, Healing, and Hope.* New York: Everystep, 2018.

Aurelius, Marcus. *Meditations.* Edited by Gregory Hays. New York: Modern Library, Random House, 2003.

Auster, Paul. *The Brooklyn Follies.* New York, NY: Henry Holt, 2006.

Berinato, Scott. "That Discomfort You're Feeling Is Grief." *Harvard Business Review*, March 23, 2020. https://hbr.org/2020/03/that-discomfort-youre-feeling-is-grief.

Blake, William. *Selected Poems of William Blake.* Edited by John Sampson. London: Oxford University Press, 1927.

Bloom, Harold, ed. *Bloom's Modern Critical Views: Henry David Thoreau.* New York, NY: Bloom's Literary Criticism, 2007.

Bodian, Stephan. *Meditation for Dummies.* Hoboken, NJ: Wiley, 2016.

Brook, Noel, and Pamela Blair. *I Wasn't Ready to Say Goodbye: Surviving, Coping and Healing after the Sudden Death of a Loved One.* Naperville, IL: Sourcebooks, 2008.

Campbell, Joseph. *The Hero with a Thousand Faces.* Novato, CA: New World Library, 2008.

Carver, Raymond. "What the Doctor Said." *ArtBeat* (blog). Humanities at University of Toronto Medicine. Originally published in *Atlantic Monthly Press*, 1989. Posted October 12, 2014. https://utmedhumanities.wordpress.com/2014/10/12/what-the-doctor-said-raymond-carver/.

Chandler, Raymond. *The Simple Art of Murder.* New York, NY: Houghton Mifflin, 1950.

Chbosky, Stephen. *The Perks of Being a Wallflower*. New York: Simon & Schuster, 1999.

Chödrön, Pema. *Welcoming the Unwelcome: Wholehearted Living in a Brokenhearted World*. Boulder, CO: Shambhala, 2019.

———. *When Things Fall Apart: Heart Advice for Difficult Times*. Boulder, CO: Shambhala, 1997.

Coelho, Paulo. *Warrior of the Light: A Manual*. London: HarperCollins, 2002.

Conroy, Pat. *My Reading Life*. New York: Nan A. Talese/Doubleday, 2010.

Dickerson, John. "Spare a Moment for Sorrow." *Atlantic*, March 29, 2020.   https://www.theatlantic.com/ideas/archive/2020/03/the -grieving-world/609013.

Dossey, Larry. *Healing Words: The Power of Prayer and the Practice of Medicine*. New York: HarperCollins, 1993.

Epictetus. *Enchiridion*. Mineola, NY: Dover. 2004.

Erdrich, Louise. *LaRose: A Novel*. New York: Harper Perennial, 2016.

———. *The Painted Drum*. New York: Harper Perennial, 2005.

Fitzgerald, Helen. *The Grieving Teen: A Guide for Teenagers and Their Friends*. New York: Fireside, 2000.

Frankl, Viktor. *Man's Search for Meaning*. Boston: Beacon Press, 2006.

Gibran, Kahlil. *The Prophet*. New York: Knopf, 1923.

Gilbert, Elizabeth. *Big Magic: Creative Living beyond Fear*. New York: Riverhead Books, 2015.

Gootman, Marilyn E. *When a Friend Dies: A Book for Teens about Grieving and Healing*. 3rd ed. Minneapolis, MN: Free Spirit, 2019.

Grollman, Earl A. *Straight Talk about Death for Teenagers: How to Cope with Losing Someone You Love*. Boston: Beacon, 1993.

Halifax, Joan. *Being with Dying: Cultivating Compassion and Fearlessness in the Presence of Death*. Boulder, CO: Shambhala, 2009.

Hanh, Thich Nhat, and Lilian Cheung. *Savor: Mindful Eating, Mindful Life*. New York: HarperCollins, 2010.

Harris, Dan. *10% Happier: How I Tamed the Voice in My Head, Reduced Stress without Losing My Edge, and Found Self-Help That Actually Works—A True Story.* New York: HarperCollins, 2014.

Harris, Sam. *The End of Faith.* New York: Norton, 2005.

————. "The Waking Up Course—A Lesson on Gratitude." Sam Harris Channel. Posted November 21, 2018. YouTube video, 3:19. https://youtu.be/2CbI0WOcUGo.

————. *Waking Up: A Guide to Spirituality without Religion.* New York: Simon & Schuster, 2014.

Hemingway, Ernest. *A Farewell to Arms.* New York, NY: Scribner, 1929.

Heshmat, Shahram. "Music, Emotion, and Well-Being." *Psychology Today,* August 25, 2019. https://www.psychologytoday.com/us/blog/science-choice/201908/music-emotion-and-well-being.

Hickman, Martha W. *Healing after Loss: Daily Meditations for Working through Grief.* New York: William Morrow, 1994.

Hughes, Lynne B. *You Are Not Alone: Teens Talk about Life after the Loss of a Parent.* New York: Scholastic, 2005.

HUMAN: The Movie. GoodPlanet Foundation. Accessed October 28, 2019. http://www.human-themovie.org/.

Karydes, Megy. "De-stress with Forest Therapy." Next Avenue. January 27, 2020. https://www.nextavenue.org/great-outdoors/.

Kessler, David. *Finding Meaning: The Sixth Stage of Grief.* New York: Scribner, 2019.

————. *Visions, Trips, and Crowded Rooms.* Carlsbad, CA: Hay House, 2010.

Kübler-Ross, Elisabeth, and David Kessler. *On Grief & Grieving: Finding the Meaning of Grief through the Five Stages of Loss.* New York: Scribner, 2014.

Lal, Tara. *Standing on My Brother's Shoulders: Making Peace with Grief and Suicide.* London: Watkins, 2015.

Lamott, Anne. *Bird by Bird: Some Instructions on Writing and Life.* New York: Pantheon Books, 1994.

Mahoney, Blair. *Poetry Reloaded.* Cambridge: Cambridge University Press, 2009.

Marchese, David. "Things Can Keep Getting Scarier: He Can Help You Cope." *New York Times Magazine*, April 11, 2020. https://www.nytimes.com/interactive/2020/04/13/magazine/jack-kornfield-mindfulness.html.

Márquez, Gabriel García. *Love in the Time of Cholera*. New York, NY: Alfred A. Knopf, 1988.

Martin, Dianne, ed. *You Are Not Alone*. Portland, OR: Inkwater, 2019.

McCarthy, Cormac. *The Road*. New York: Knopf, 2006.

McDowell, Adele Ryan. *Making Peace with Suicide: A Book of Hope, Understanding, and Comfort*. Riverside, CT: White Flower, 2015.

Mendoza, Marilyn A. "Dreams and Grief." *Psychology Today*, April 8, 2019. https://www.psychologytoday.com/us/blog/understanding-grief/201904/dreams-and-grief.

Merritt, James. *52 Weeks through the Psalms*. Eugene, OR: Harvest House Publishers, 2017.

Nakadate, Neil, ed. *Robert Penn Warren: Critical Perspectives*. Lexington, KY: University Press of Kentucky, 1981.

Nietzsche, Friedrich. *Thus Spoke Zarathustra*. Edited by Thomas Common. New York, NY: Modern Library, 1917.

O'Brien, Tim. *Dad's Maybe Book*. Boston: Houghton Mifflin Harcourt, 2019.

Oliver, Mary. *Why I Wake Early*. Boston: Beacon, 2005.

Peterson, Jordan. *Maps of Meaning: The Architecture of Belief*. Abingdon: Taylor and Francis, 1999.

Pratchett, Terry. *Going Postal*. New York: HarperCollins, 2004.

Pressfield, Steven. *Gates of Fire: An Epic Novel of the Battle of Thermopylae*. New York, NY: Doubleday, 1998.

Redglass Pictures. "Ken Burns: On Story." Redglass Pictures. Posted December 18, 2015. YouTube video, 5:21. https://youtu.be/VlZYgPllKNU.

Robbins, Jim. "How Immersing Yourself in Nature Benefits Your Health." PBS.org. January 13, 2020. https://www.pbs.org/newshour/health/how-immersing-yourself-in-nature-benefits-your-health.

Schuurman, Donna. *Never the Same: Coming to Terms with the Death of a Parent.* New York: St. Martin's, 2003.

Seneca, Lucius Annaeus. *Minor Dialogues.* Edited by Aubrey Stewart. London: Chiswick Press, 1889.

Thompson, Lawrance, and R. H. Winnick. *Robert Frost: A Biography.* New York, NY: Holt, Rinehart and Winston, 1981.

Villarosa, Clara. *The Words of African-American Heroes.* New York, NY: Newmarket Press, 2011.

Wolfelt, Alan. *Healing Your Grieving Heart for Teens: 100 Practical Ideas.* Fort Collins, CO: Companion, 2001.

INDEX

ABOUT THE AUTHOR

Joe Jansen's curiosity into the nature of grief and how we embrace life in the face of loss began when a young friend died of leukemia. His interest in understanding death as a part of life led him to four years working with dying people and their families as a hospice volunteer. As a writer, Joe has worked as a medical and technical writer; has been an editor of trade, computer, and history books; and has written for regional, history, and outdoor magazines. Joe is a Marine Corps veteran and a graduate of Indiana University. He lives in central Indiana.